10/10.
35.00
00

World of Dance

Latin and Caribbean Dance

World of Dance

African Dance, Second Edition

Asian Dance, Second Edition

Ballet, Second Edition

European Dance:
Ireland, Poland, Spain, and Greece, Second Edition

Latin and Caribbean Dance

Middle Eastern Dance, Second Edition

Modern Dance, Second Edition

Popular Dance: From Ballroom to Hip-Hop

Latin and Caribbean Dance

Margaret Musmon

Consulting editor:
Elizabeth A. Hanley,
Associate Professor
Emerita of Kinesiology,
Penn State University

Foreword by
Jacques D'Amboise,
Founder of the National
Dance Institute

CHELSEA HOUSE
PUBLISHERS
An imprint of Infobase Publishing

Chelsea House
An imprint of Infobase Publishing
132 West 31st Street
New York NY 10001

Library of Congress Cataloging-in-Publication Data
Musmon, Margaret.
 Latin and Caribbean dance / Margaret Musmon.
     p. cm. — (World of dance)
 Includes bibliographical references and index.
 ISBN 978-1-60413-481-0 (hardcover)
 1. Dance—Latin America—Juvenile literature. 2. Dance—Caribbean Area—Juvenile literature. I. Title. II. Series.
 GV1596.5.M87 2010
 793.3'198—dc22   2009053492

Chelsea House books are available at special discounts when purchased in bulk quantities for businesses, associations, institutions, or sales promotions. Please call our Special Sales Department in New York at (212) 967-8800 or (800) 322-8755.

You can find Chelsea House on the World Wide Web at
http://www.chelseahouse.com

Text design by Kerry Casey
Cover design by Alicia Post
Composition by EJB Publishing Services
Cover printed by Bang Printing, Brainerd, MN
Book printed and bound by Bang Printing, Brainerd, MN
Date printed: May 2010
Printed in the United States of America

10 9 8 7 6 5 4 3 2 1

This book is printed on acid-free paper.

All links and Web addresses were checked and verified to be correct at the time of publication. Because of the dynamic nature of the Web, some addresses and links may have changed since publication and may no longer be valid.

CONTENTS

Introduction 7
by Consulting Editor Elizabeth A. Hanley,
Associate Professor Emerita of Kinesiology,
Pennsylvania State University

Foreword 10
by Jacques D'Amboise,
Founder of the National Dance Institute

1 Roots of Caribbean and
   Latin American Music and Dance 15

2 Dances of Cuba 26

3 Dances of Hispaniola:
   Dominican Republic 41

4 Dances of Hispaniola: Haiti 50

5 Argentine Tango 58

6 Dances of Brazil: Samba 70

7 Dances of Brazil: Capoeira 78

8 Salsa 85

Chronology 93

Notes 98

Glossary 100

Bibliography   109
Further Resources   110
Picture Credits   113
Index   114
About the Author   119
About the Consulting Editor   120

INTRODUCTION

The world of dance is yours to enjoy! Dance has existed from time immemorial. It has been an integral part of celebrations and rituals, a means of communication with gods and among humans, and a basic source of enjoyment and beauty.

Dance is a fundamental element of human behavior and has evolved over the years from primitive movement of the earliest civilizations to traditional ethnic or folk styles, to the classical ballet and modern dance genres popular today. The term *dance* is broad and, therefore, not limited to the genres noted above. In the twenty-first century, dance includes ballroom, jazz, tap, aerobics, and a myriad of other movement activities. The joy derived from participating in dance of any genre and the physical activity required provide the opportunity for the pursuit of a healthy lifestyle in today's world.

The richness of cultural traditions observed in the ethnic, or folk, dance genre offers the participant, as well as the spectator, insight into the customs, geography, dress, and religious nature of a particular people. Originally passed on from one generation to the next, many ethnic, or folk, dances continue to evolve as our civilization and society change. From these quaint beginnings of traditional dance, a new genre emerged as a way to appeal to the upper level of society: ballet. This new form of dance rose quickly in popularity and remains so today. The genre of ethnic, or folk, dance continues to be an important part of ethnic communities throughout the United States, particularly in large cities.

When the era of modern dance emerged as a contrast and a challenge to the rigorously structured world of ballet, it was not readily accepted as an art form. Modern dance was interested in the communication of emotional experiences—through basic movement, as well as uninhibited movement—not through the academic tradition of ballet masters. Modern dance, however, found its aficionados and is a popular art form today.

No dance form is permanent, definitive, or ultimate. Changes occur, but the basic element of dance endures. Dance is for all people. One need only recall that dance needs neither common race nor common language for communication; it has been, and remains, a universal means of communication.

The WORLD OF DANCE series provides a starting point for readers interested in learning about ethnic, or folk, dances of world cultures, as well as the art forms of ballet and modern dance. This series features an overview of the development of these dance genres, from a historical perspective to a practical one. Highlighting specific cultures, their dance steps and movements, and their customs and traditions underscores the importance of these fundamental elements for the reader. Ballet and modern dance—more recent artistic dance genres—are explored in detail as well, giving the reader a comprehensive knowledge of the past, present, and potential future of each dance form.

The one fact that each reader should remember is that dance has always been, and always will be, a form of communication. This is its legacy to the world.

***

In this volume, Professor Margaret Musmon explores the history of dance on the islands of the Dominican Republic, Haiti, and Cuba and in the South American countries of Argentina and Brazil. She also describes the music and dance of indigenous Indian cultures, an important part of the history of dance. This volume includes European, African, and Creole influences on dance and describes the popular celebration of Carnival (Karnival) in detail. The role of religion takes on special significance in many of the dances highlighted in *Latin and Caribbean Dance*, from Catholicism to voodoo. Politics also played a definitive role in shaping and popularizing these dances.

Examples of specific dances discussed in this volume are the rumba and its variations, the son, the bolero, the mambo, the cha-cha-chá, the merengue, the salsa, the tango and milonga, the samba, the maxixe, the bossa nova, and the capoeira. Each dance has distinguishing characteristics, which Professor Musmon presents to the reader in an interesting fashion.

Latin dance clubs in New York, Miami, Havana, and San Juan are popular today; Argentine tango lessons are on the rise; and International Salsa Congresses (Colombia is a transnational hub for salsa!) are gaining popularity throughout the world.

—Elizabeth A. Hanley
Associate Professor Emerita of Kinesiology at
Pennsylvania State University

FOREWORD

In song and dance, man expresses himself as a member of a higher community. He forgets how to walk and speak and is on the way into flying into the air, dancing. . . . His very gestures express enchantment.

—Friedrich Nietzsche

In a conversation with George Balanchine [one of the twentieth century's most famous choreographers and the cofounder of the New York City Ballet] discussing the definition of dance, we evolved the following description: "Dance is an expression of time and space, using the control of movement and gesture to communicate."

Dance is central to the human being's expression of emotion. Every time we shake someone's hand, lift a glass in a toast, wave good-bye, or applaud a performer, we are doing a form of dance. We live in a universe of time and space, and dance is an art form invented by human beings to express and convey emotions. Dance is profound.

There are melodies that, when played, will cause your heart to droop with sadness for no known reason. Or a rousing jig or mazurka will have your foot tapping in an accompanying rhythm, seemingly beyond your control. The emotions, contacted through music, spur the body to react physically. Our bodies have just been programmed to express emotions. We dance for many reasons: for religious rituals from the most ancient times; for dealing with sadness, tearfully swaying and holding hands at a wake; for celebrating weddings, joyfully spinning in circles; for entertainment; for dating and mating. How many millions of couples through the ages have said, "We met at a dance"? But most of all, we dance for joy, often exclaiming, "How I love to dance!" Oh, the JOY OF DANCE!

I was teaching dance at a boarding school for emotionally disturbed children, ages 9 through 16. They were participating with 20 other schools in the National Dance Institute's (NDI) year-round program. The boarding school children had been traumatized in frightening and mind-boggling ways. There were a dozen students in my class, and the average attention span may have been 15 seconds—which made for a raucous bunch. This was a tough class.

One young boy, an 11-year-old, was an exception. He never took his eyes off of me for the 35 minutes of the dance class, and they were blazing blue eyes—electric, set in a chalk-white face. His body was slim, trim, superbly proportioned, and he stood arrow-straight. His lips were clamped in a rigid, determined line as he learned and executed every dance step with amazing skill. His concentration was intense despite the wild cavorting, noise, and otherwise disruptive behavior supplied by his fellow classmates.

At the end of class, I went up to him and said, "Wow, can you dance. You're great! What's your name?"

Those blue eyes didn't blink. Then he parted his rigid lips and bared his teeth in a grimace that may have been a smile. He had a big hole where his front teeth should be. I covered my shock and didn't let it show. Both top and bottom incisors had been worn away by his continual grinding and rubbing of them together. One of the supervisors of the school rushed over to me and said, "Oh, his name is Michael. He's very intelligent, but he doesn't speak."

I heard Michael's story from the supervisor. Apparently, when he was a toddler in his playpen, he witnessed his father shooting his mother; then putting the gun to his own head, the father killed himself. It was close to three days before the neighbors broke in to find the dead and swollen bodies of his parents. The dehydrated and starving little boy was stuck in his playpen, sitting in his own filth. The orphaned Michael disappeared into the foster care system, eventually ending up in the boarding school. No one had ever heard him speak.

In the ensuing weeks of dance class, I built and developed choreography for Michael and his classmates. In the spring, they were scheduled to dance in a spectacular NDI show called *The Event of the Year*. At the boarding school, I used Michael as the leader and as a model for the others and began welding all of the kids together, inventing a vigorous and energetic dance to utilize their explosive energy. It took awhile, but they were coming together, little by little over the months. And through all that time, the best in the class—the determined and concentrating Michael—never spoke.

That spring, dancers from the 22 different schools with which the NDI had dance programs were scheduled to come together at Madison Square Garden for *The Event of the Year*. There would be more than 2,000 dancers, a symphony orchestra, a jazz orchestra, a chorus, Broadway stars, narrators, and Native American Indian drummers. There was scenery that was the length of an entire city block and visiting guest children from six foreign countries coming to dance with our New York City children. All of these elements had to come together and fit into a spectacular performance, with only one day of rehearsal. The foremost challenge was how to get 2,000 dancing children on stage for the opening number.

At NDI, we have developed a system called "the runs." First, we divide the stage into a grid with colored lines making the outlines of box shapes, making a mosaic of patterns and shapes on the stage floor. Each outlined box holds a class from one of the schools, which consists of 15 to 30 children. Then, we add various colored lines as tracks, starting offstage and leading to the boxes. The dancers line up in the wings, hallways, and various holding areas on either side of the stage. At the end of the overture, they burst onto the stage, running and leaping and following their colored tracks to their respective boxes, where they explode into the opening dance number.

We had less than three minutes to accomplish "the runs." It's as if a couple of dozen trains coming from different places and traveling on different tracks all arrived at a station at the same time, safely pulling into their allotted spaces. But even before starting, it would take us almost an hour just to get the dancers lined up in the correct holding areas offstage, ready to make their entrance. We had scheduled one shot to rehearse the opening. It had to work the first time, or we would have to repeat everything. That would mean going into overtime at a great expense.

I gave the cue to start the number. The orchestra, singers, lights, and stagehands all commenced on cue, and the avalanche of 2,000 children was let loose on their tracks. "The runs" had begun!

After about a minute, I realized something was wrong. There was a big pileup on stage left, and children were colliding into each other and bunching up behind some obstacle. I ran over to discover the source of the problem: Michael and his classmates. He had ignored everything and led the group from his school right up front, as close to the audience as he could get. Inspiring his dancing buddies, they were a crew of leaping, contorting demons—dancing up a storm, but blocking some 600 other dancers trying to get through.

I rushed up to them, yelling, "You're in the wrong place! Back up! Back up!"

Michael—with his eyes blazing, mouth open, and legs and arms spinning in dance movements like an eggbeater—yelled out, "Oh, I am so happy! I am so happy! Thank you, Jacques! Oh, it's so good! I am so happy!"

I backed off, stunned into silence. I sat down in the first row of the audience and was joined by several of the supervisors, teachers, and chaperones from Michael's school, our mouths open in wonder. The spirit of dance had taken over Michael and his classmates. No one danced better or with more passion in the whole show that night and with Michael leading the way—the JOY OF DANCE was at work. (We went into overtime, but so what!)

—Jacques D'Amboise
Author of *Teaching the Magic of Dance*, winner of an
Academy Award for *He Makes Me Feel Like Dancin'*,
and Founder of the National Dance Institute

Roots of Caribbean and Latin American Music and Dance

Caribbean people love to dance. They strive to achieve physical and artistic mastery of their dances, and they become passionately attached to the dances they perform. Personal identity and a relationship with the spirit world are asserted through dance movements.[1]

Latin America consists of those countries in the Americas where romance languages are primarily spoken. The predominant language spoken in Latin American countries is Spanish, followed by Portuguese, which is especially predominant in Brazil. French and **Creole languages**—based upon Spanish and Portuguese—are spoken in some Caribbean countries, such as Haiti. These romance languages, all based on Latin, were spread through the Caribbean and South, Central, and North America by European conquerors from Spain, Portugal, and France. "The term *Latin America* was popularized by Napoleon III as part of his campaign to imply cultural kinship with France and to install Maximilian as emperor of Mexico."[2]

This book examines dances from three representative Caribbean nations—Cuba, the Dominican Republic, and Haiti—and from two representative South American Countries—Argentina and Brazil.

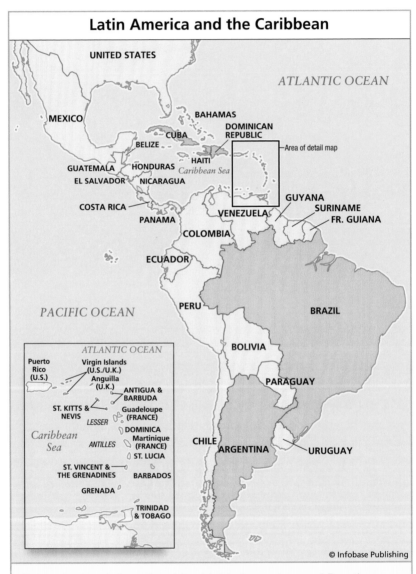

Latin America and the Caribbean

Cuba, the Dominican Republic, Haiti, Argentina, and Brazil are among the most prominent countries in which dance has a long, rich history.

INDIGENOUS MUSIC AND DANCE

The indigenous people of the Americas danced and sang to the beats of wooden drums. The identity of each culture was imprinted through the gestures made while dancing. Specialized dances sought healthy crops and bountiful harvests, celebrated rites of passage (such as the coming of age, weddings, and funerals) and preparations for war, and recorded the emotion and history of the people.

THE INDIAN CULTURE

In the fifteenth century, a socioreligious ceremony, *areíto*, was at the center of the indigenous Caribbean music of the **Amerindians**, including the **Taino (Arawak) Indians**. The musicians sang **call-and-response**-style mythical chants. Large numbers of dancers moved in concentric circles as musicians played rattles made of gourds filled with small stones (later called **maracas**), gourd scrapers, conch-shell horns, and hollowed-out logs with H-shaped tongues cut into them, called *mayohuacan*, or *at-tambor*. The absence of large mammals prevented the making of drums with skin heads.[3] The enormous Taino *areíto* dances were described as religious ceremonies in which hundreds, if not thousands, of Indians participated. They danced in unison in a circle with their arms intertwined, stepping forward and backward, and singing as a chorus while responding to the leader's phrases and repeating his or her dance steps. Simple steps were done in intricate patterns (lines, circles, and zigzags), some for both men and women and others for men or women only. The song lyrics were stories of the past that were constantly being updated, serving as an oral history and as a news broadcast. The areíto could last for many hours with the same lead singer until the story was complete, the festivities normally lasting for days.

EUROPEAN INFLUENCES

The indigenous people of the Americas were greatly influenced by the cultural contact and conflict caused by their interactions with European

For many tribes of the Caribbean region, including the Taino, dancing was an important part of religious ceremonies. In this eighteenth-century painting by American artist Benjamin West, a group of Taino Indians welcomes Christopher Columbus to what is now Cuba in 1492.

colonists from Spain, Portugal, England, and France. These influences included classical music of the era and, more important, folk and popular songs and dances of the period. Some examples are sea chanteys, hymns, marches, and, predominantly, social dances, including the quadrille, the contredanse, and the zapateo.

The **quadrille** and other "set" dances were popular throughout the Caribbean. Most were round or line dances led by a caller. Ballroom-style social dances, including the **waltz**, the **polka**, the **mazurka**, and the **schottische**, gradually became popular.

The **contredanse** was first danced in Versailles, then in the Spanish court, and afterwards in the Caribbean. During the Spanish colonization, this dance was called *contradanza*. The contredanse arrived in Haiti, while the contradanza arrived in Havana, Cuba. These "contra dances" are still widely performed. There are numerous contra dance societies throughout the world.

As these dances were performed for generations by Afro-Caribbeans, they became creolized. The European dances mixed with the

(continues on page 22)

THE TRIANGLE OF TRADE

The Triangle of Trade brought African slaves to the Americas to work on the plantations. Side one of the triangle was the export of European goods to Africa. Many African kings and merchants were involved in the slave trade and would receive European-made commodities, including guns, ammunition, and other factory-made wares.

The second side of the triangle sent enslaved Africans across the Atlantic Ocean to North America, South America, and the Caribbean Islands once the Europeans had discovered the New World.

The third side of the triangle was the shipment of goods, including cotton, sugar, tobacco, molasses, and rum, to Europe from the Americas. These products were produced on plantations worked by African slaves.

CARNIVAL

The origins of **Carnival** date back to ancient Greece and Rome in springtime festivals of the gods of wine, Dionysus and Bacchus. Influenced by Catholicism, the festivals became times of revelry, dance, masquerade, processions, and parades in the days leading up to Ash Wednesday, which is 40 days before Easter. The word *carnival* itself is thought to derive from the Latin words *carne* and *vale,* "a farewell to meat," signaling the Catholic custom of abstaining from meat during Lent.

Throughout Latin America, Carnival has many similarities. Begun in the early years of European colonization as ritual celebrations, the colonists' slaves added elements from their African homelands. African customs of wearing both costumes and masks made of feathers, of dancing in circular processions around villages, and of drumming all add to present-day Carnival. Masks, in addition to disguising their wearers from supernatural beings, can also depict or capture the attention of the spirit world.

The Carnival in Rio de Janeiro, Brazil, dates from 1840 and evolved from a simple marching parade into the famous **Samba** Parade in the Sambadrome Stadium. The Carnival in Rio de Janeiro is organized by samba schools that first appeared in 1928; they plan, nearly a year in advance, the theme, multicolored costumes, elaborate floats, and trappings and music that will represent them in the Carnival. Many thousands of dancers, singers, and drummers parade through the stadium. The samba is a distinctly Brazilian form of music that includes elements of the Angolan **semba**, the Cuban **habanera**, and other European and African musical traditions, principally those of the numerous black immigrants who arrived from Bahia after the elimination of slavery in Brazil in 1888.

The Carnival in Rio de Janeiro is characterized by lavish, expensive floats and costumes and the samba schools' parade, whereas the Carnival in Brazil's Salvador da Bahia is a people's carnival with everyone dancing in the streets for weeks before the Lenten season begins, starting at midday and lasting until the early morning hours.

The most famous Carnival in Argentina, at Gualeguaychú, resembles the Rio de Janeiro festival with dancers, bands, colorful floats, and state-of-the-art productions. Tickets to view this carnival in the Corsódromo are sold in advance. In Buenos Aires, more than a hundred street bands participate in some 40 parades each February.

Haiti's Carnival celebrations begin on the Sunday after Epiphany (January 6) and last until Ash Wednesday. The

(continues)

Since 1928, samba schools have been an integral part of Rio de Janeiro's Carnival celebration, which takes place each year during the four days prior to Lent. Here, Academicos do Salgueiro samba school dancers perform along the Sambadrome during Rio's Carnival celebration in 2009.

◇◇

(continued)

rara bands also continue festivities on the Sundays of Lent and in the week before Easter.

In the Dominican Republic, Carnival is a countrywide, month-long event ending on February 27, the Dominican Republic's independence day. Costumes range from bodies painted or decorated in papers, rags, or mud to the more elaborately costumed dancing girls and devils (***diablos cojuelos***) of every imaginable shape and color.

Carnival in Cuba, once as elaborate and extravagant as any, was shifted to July under the Castro regime to coincide with the end of the sugarcane harvest and to celebrate the triumph of the Cuban Revolution of 1959. Cancelled in the early 1990s in a severe economy, some of the festivities have been recently restored.

◇◇

(continued from page 19)

African rhythms, and each dance assimilated its own characteristic **syncopation** and other distinctly local features.

AFRICAN INFLUENCES ON LATIN AMERICAN DANCE

Slaves brought few belongings as evidence of their African culture, but the **polyrhythms** of their music and dance have had a lasting effect on the music and dance of the New World. The most distinct and frequently noted feature of African music is its emphasis on rhythm. The interest and complexity of the rhythm come from regular beats (silent or heard) and offbeat accents. This feature is known as syncopation.

Congo *(Kongo-Angolian)* music and dance were an important part of social gatherings in most Caribbean and early Latin American nations.

This very percussive and frequently sensuous dance involved flirtations between a man and a woman. The dancers bent forward, often very low, and executed jumps and powerful movements with their entire bodies. Body parts were isolated, allowing the torso and limbs to move independently. Movements were initiated by the hips, which swung side to side or gyrated in circles.

A prevalent feature of African music and dance is singing call-and-response chants. These chants are well suited to communal performance or group participation. This feature is typical of classless societies that lack occupational distinctions between performers and spectators. Soloists and specialists have roles in the music and dances. At the same time, it is customary for most members of a community to participate by dancing, singing, clapping, or playing instruments. This custom fortifies the concept that music and dance talent is innate in everyone, not only in the gifted, though to different degrees. This collective participation, which often begins as early as a baby can be carried on its dancing mother's back, leads to the development of talent to a greater extent than that which occurs in other societies.

Wherever African slaves were brought in the Americas, dance developed based on African rhythmic concepts in conjunction with European influences and, in some places, Native American dances.[4] Indigenous music and dance, however, were less influential in the history of Latin American popular dance.[5]

Many of the dances of Latin America and the Caribbean began as commemorations by the African slaves when their captors forced them to emigrate from their native Africa. The dances were performed as rituals reminding the slaves of their heritage, of their spirituality and spirit worship, of celebrations of individual rites of passage, of communal celebrations, and of festivals of tribes and of nations.

The upper European classes considered the dances of the African slaves vulgar and unworthy of their joining in these ritualistic dances. Likewise, the Africans felt that European dances that involved touching were vulgar. As these African and European dances evolved, elements from each were combined to form the popular dances of the twentieth century. As the **tango**, for example, became a dance that evolved among the lower classes and then caught on in more respectable quarters and was danced by more upscale dancers, its popularity spread through the entire society and beyond. This spreading of popularity is also true of the **maxixe**, the **samba**, the **cha-cha-chá**, the **merengue**, the **salsa**, and others as these dances achieved widespread popularity in the twentieth century.

In the 1940s, researchers began codifying Caribbean island **folkloric** dance to create a body of work for the stage. These pieces became repertoires of national dances and have become important bases of history and choreography. This activity has led to the preservation of traditional dances while modern Latin dances remain in transition.

Scholars have commented on the extent of compatibility between African and European music and dance. Two- and three-part harmony is common in African and European music. Protestant hymns included call and response corresponding to African song-and-dance technique. The Spanish and French colonists and many African communities

KATHERINE DUNHAM

When you have faith in something, it's your reason to be alive and to fight for it.

—Katherine Dunham

Katherine Dunham received a Julius Rosenwald Fund fellowship in 1936 to study the dance forms of the Caribbean. She conducted extensive fieldwork in Cuba, Haiti, Jamaica, Martinique, and Trinidad during the 1930s. Dunham made significant contributions to the discipline of dance anthropology and developed the first African American concert dance technique. Combining her two interests, anthropology and dance, she linked the function and form of Caribbean dance and ritual to their African sources. These experiences changed the focus of her life and career. Dunham's fieldwork provided the nucleus for future research and began a lifelong involvement with the people and dance of Haiti. She divided her time between Haiti and celebrated seasonal carnivals with festive music and dance. In addition, succeeding generations passed on European folk music and dances, as has been done with African dance, through performance. It was as customary for Africans to dance in lines as it was for Europeans to dance in lines in the European contredanse.

Dance is almost always inseparable from music. Caribbean and Latin American dance and music developed together. Either the dance evolved to fit the music, or the music was transformed to accompany the dance.

The following chapters highlight dances indigenous to Cuba, the Dominican Republic, Haiti, Argentina, and Brazil; their adaptation through European and African influences; and their development in the modern world.

---

the United States and become a priestess in the vodoun religion. Dunham wrote three books about her observations in Haiti: *Journey to Accompong* (1946), *The Dances of Haiti* (her master's thesis, published in 1947), and *Island Possessed* (1969), underscoring how African religions and rituals adapted to the New World.[6]

A Brief Listing of Katherine Dunham's Awards and Achievements

1979   The Katherine Dunham Museum and Children's Workshop opened in East St. Louis, Illinois; the Katherine Dunham Gala was held at Carnegie Hall in New York, where she was awarded the prestigious Albert Schweitzer Music Award.

1983   Presented the Kennedy Center Honors Award; awarded an honorary doctorate degree from Spellman College in Atlanta, Georgia.

2000   Named one of "America's Irreplaceable Dance Treasures" by the Dance Heritage Coalition

Dances
of Cuba

Cuba, the largest and most populated Caribbean island, was claimed for Spain by Christopher Columbus in 1492 and settled in 1511 by Diego Velázquez de Cuéllar, making it the oldest European settlement in the New World. New Cuban dance forms appeared with each original Cuban music form, including the **son**, the **rumba**, the **mambo**, the **danzón**, and the cha-cha-chá. The major difference between Cuban and non-Hispanic Caribbean dance structure is in the syncopated foot pattern: "short, short, long, short, short, long" or "long, short, short, long, short, short," which moves the dancers through space. Dance foot patterns of other islands often consist of alternating walking steps: "one, two" or "walk, walk" basic steps. In most modern Caribbean dances, remnants of Cuban dance are evident. This carry-over is due to the early settlement of Cuba and later exploration of the other islands.

INDIGENOUS DANCE OF CUBA

The Taino (Arawak) and **Ciboney Indians** were native to Cuba. By the 1600s, they had disappeared along with their language, music, and culture.

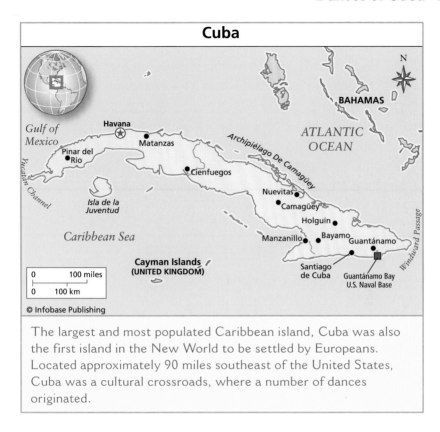

Cuba

The largest and most populated Caribbean island, Cuba was also the first island in the New World to be settled by Europeans. Located approximately 90 miles southeast of the United States, Cuba was a cultural crossroads, where a number of dances originated.

We know about Cuban indigenous dances through the **conquistadores'** descriptions in their journals. Though the indigenous music and dances no longer exist, Cubans allude to them in contemporary work.

EUROPEAN INFLUENCES

Lyrics are sung in the Spanish language using *décima* form, a Spanish song structure based on a 10-syllable line within a 10-line stanza. The guitar and other stringed instruments used for playing early Cuban dance music were Spanish. The Spanish dance style features an elongated, lifted upper body. The feet move in a **zapateo** (stamping) style of percussive movement in rhythmic patterns. The arms move in circular patterns as the hips sway. These were all components of what was to become Cuban, not Spanish, music and dance. Zapateo is also a lively couple's dance from the colonial period featuring foot stamping to syncopated music.[7]

French colonials who had left either Haiti during the Haitian Revolution (1791–1803) or French Louisiana as it was coming under U.S. control (1803) introduced the look of French court dance (quadrilles and **minuets**) on half toe (with weight on the ball of the foot). The form danced most frequently in Cuba was the contredanse (**contradanza Francesa**). Couples, often in four pairs, paraded, promenaded, and crossed the floor in complex patterns, infrequently touching fingers or hands.

AFRICAN INFLUENCES

Cabildos (African ethnic or fraternal associations) were allowed to meet, practice, and preserve their customs in Cuba, enabling traditions of each African group to be exhibited through their unique music and dance.

A Haitian culture was developed by enslaved Africans and African Americans. Their dances were unique because they were accompanied by the emerging Creole French language. These differed from other African forms because they resembled European court dances and were performed to drums by people of African heritage. "In reality, their dance/music was a distinct mixture of colonists' European court imitations (of contredanse, quadrilles, minuets, and **cotillions**) and African imitations of these colonial forms. This music/dance tradition continues today as *tumba Francesa*, or French Drum—intact from the late 1700s to the present!"[8]

The four rhythms that compose Afro-Cuban music and dance traditions are as follows:

1. Congo rhythms from Central Africa form the foundation for community social dance. Congo-Angolian music and dance are associated with **Palo**. This Congolese-derived Cuban religion is based on worshiping ancestors and attributes human form and behavior to Afro-Caribbean deities. Simple rhythms are played on a single-headed *ngoma* drum. Palo dances are more vigorous than the **Santería** dances described below.

2. *Arará* rhythms come from countries bordering the Bight of Benin, a bay forming the western part of the Gulf of Guinea and extending from the mouth of the Volta River to the mouth of the Niger River in West Africa. This area was known as the Slave Coast during the eighteenth century. Arará rhythms are played on drums that are cylindrical or tube shaped and with sticks by drummers who often stand while leaning the drums on a bench. In arará dances, shoulder movements are emphasized. The dancers may bend over or stand as they continuously pulsate their shoulders up and down or push them backward, executing complex movements throughout their bodies.

3. **Carabalí** rhythms from the Calabar region in Africa are the most distinctive music and dance tradition in Cuba. In Carabalí dances, smooth lunges are alternated with standing postures in which the dancer is high on the toes with a pulled-up torso. *Abakuá* are male-only ethnic and religious brotherhoods from the Calabar region. They practice the only surviving mask tradition in Cuba. During religious ceremonies, dancers reenact their mythical history. The most distinctive figure in Abakuá dance is the little devil (*diablito*) in a hooded costume darting around with a whisk broom.

4. **Yoruba** rhythms from what is now southwestern Nigeria are known for identifiable movement sequences and gestures that represent divine personalities, or *orishas*. Yoruba dances and music are performed as offerings to the orishas. The lyrical dance movements make the dancer appear to wave vertically, starting with the pelvic area up through the core, shoulders, neck, and head. Santería (*Regla de Ocha*) is a Yoruba-based religion with a thin veil of Roman Catholicism. A *bembé* is a dance event associated with the Afro-Cuban Santería religion. Rhythms are beaten by a trio of drummers on two-headed *batá* drums, which are played with both hands as the drums rest across the drummers' laps. During this dance, the Santería altar is strewn with blood and feathers from a chicken sacrifice. The participants, mostly women, dance in a circle in a joyful way; others sing a call-and-response chant. As the drumming

Shoulder movements are emphasized in arará dances; dancers pulsate their shoulders up and down or push them backward and execute complex movements throughout their bodies. Here, Cuban dancers perform the arará dance in Jovellanos, Cuba.

reaches a frenetic pace, two of the dancers stiffen, their eyes glaze over, and they collapse into the arms of other dancers. They have been possessed by Elegba, the Santería god of crossroads, who dances in red and black clothing, holding a tree branch. They spend several hours in a trance, remembering nothing of this experience when they awake.[9]

HABANERA

The **habanera** evolved in the early nineteenth century from contradanza, which the Spanish adapted from the French contredanse of the eighteenth century, an adaptation of seventeenth-century English country dances, or contra dance. French planters fleeing the slave rebellion of the 1790s in Haiti introduced the contredanse into Cuba. The habanera had a mild Afro-Caribbean syncopation, an eight-beat rhythm divided into 3-3-2. Cubans prized the habanera as a local Creole invention. In the nineteenth century, Cuban habanera captivated audiences in Europe and was seen in operas such as *Carmen*. It also influenced ragtime music in American jazz.

THE CUBAN DANZÓN

Bandleader Miguel Faílde composed the first danzón score in 1879. In the late 1800s, danzón emerged and was considered the national dance of Cuba until the 1930s. Its heritage stems from the French contredanse and the Haitian tumba francesa as evidenced by the upright posture and the couples who danced facing each other. As the dance developed, couples danced not merely facing each other, but with the woman placing her finger tips on the palm of the man's hands. Dancers alternated between dancing in this close position for eight measures and promenading while talking to other couples, fanning themselves, or resting for eight measures. This structure of walking elegantly to the music (***paseo***) came from Spain.

The danzón rhythm contained five pulses (***cinquillo***) within a three-beat structure, which is related to the development of the Cuban ***clave***. Danzón had a brilliant syncopation between the dancers and musicians, allowing the dancers to emphasize the syncopation of the clave. Danzón was born in Cuba, but it also had African roots in the use of kettledrums. Furthermore, the rhythm of danzón is very much like the tango rhythm that Africans dance.

CLAVE

Cubans discovered that striking together a pair of cylindrical wooden sticks—made from hardwood (ebony or hard pine) used for ship building—one inch in diameter and eight inches in length produced a metallic sound that rises above all other instruments. They called them claves. The claves keep all instruments and their improvisations within a repeated pattern. In two-three clave rhythm, "one, two—one, two, three" is played repeatedly. In three-two clave rhythm, "one, two, three—one, two" is played repeatedly. Claves direct the dancers' footsteps. Claves were first heard in public in Cuban son music.

SON

The son originated in Cuba as a mixture of Spanish and Afro-Cuban elements. In the beginning, the European features were strongest. As the son became more popular in Cuba, the Afro-Cuban features became more prominent. Around 1917, the Cuban son appeared in Havana, achieving commercial appeal while maintaining its barrio flavor. The son had the same elements as the danzón; the difference was in its form of accompaniment by percussion and rhythmic instruments only, which made the rhythm prominent. Cinquillo rhythm, five pulses within three beats, was the first part of the son clave. Other instruments were the **palmadas** (Flamenco hand claps); the **güiros**; the maracas; and the guitar and its offshoot, a Cuban innovation called the **tres**. These instruments accompanied the son from its inception until 1930, when other instruments were added. The mambo, cha-cha-chá, and salsa are variations of the son. The popularity of the son over the centuries has encouraged improvisation in movement and music.

BOLERO

Bolero, a style of love song, was written and danced throughout Latin America. It was a genre that unified Latin Americans as a culture without regard to countries and borders. The bolero, a slow romantic music played and danced in cinquillo syncopation, like a very slow song, developed in Cuba around the turn of the twentieth century. It became a popular form of music and dance throughout Latin America by the 1920s. This "dance of love" came to the United States in the 1930s. The original Spanish bolero was played in 3/4 time while the Cuban bolero was played in 2/4 and later 4/4 time. It was originally danced by a single female and later by couples.

CUBAN RUMBA

The Cuban rumba evolved in the late 1800s through the interaction of slaves from different African regions and from African Americans and Europeans. It is not a transplant from Africa but a distinctly Cuban creation. The rumba had all of the same ingredients as the son: Spanish and African languages, décima-derived lyrics in call-and-response patterns, and polyrhythms in both music and movement structures. The rumba, however, had a more pronounced emphasis on rhythm and the anticipation of improvisation in both the music and the dance. This became more complex and required an understanding of the culture in order to appreciate it. It was expected that a rumba continues until all singers completed their improvised lyrics, or **cantos**, which were often about love, politics, local events, and citizens or about forms of social resistance. Likewise, all dancers displayed their talent before the rumba ended.

The rumba was accompanied by claves, drums, shakers, and human voices. The **montuno** portion of the rumba is a call-and-response pattern. When the montuno starts, a couple begins to dance. The woman shyly avoids the man as he playfully tries to capture her. She dances gracefully around the man who, without touching her, performs improvised steps and gestures around her. He pretends to take no notice of her, then to entice her. Finally, he performs a **vacunano**, which is a pelvic thrust, kick, or swat aimed toward her groin. The dance is fun; its humor, sophistication, and variety of movement keep it from being vulgar.[10]

The goals of the rumba are to enhance the clave rhythm, to dance in perfect time with absolute syncopation, and to use every movable body part, especially the hips. The simplest form of rumba pattern is danced by stepping to the side with the right foot, then returning to a position with the two feet together. This pattern is then repeated on the left and continues, alternating feet.

The rumba originated in Cuba during the late 1800s, but performances of the dance were often restricted because it was considered dangerous and lewd by white Cubans. Here, a female rumba dancer in blue costume performs bare-footed during Santiago's Carnival celebrations.

There are three types of rumba with contrasting tempi—slow, medium, and fast— each one having different recognizable clave rhythms. The first two are performed only by a couple, one woman and one man, who must exhibit absolute creativity danced with a complete comprehension of clave. They are watched by all spectators and thereby take responsibility for representing all men or women in the community. They dance together, but apart in a circle, exhibiting the lowest knee bends and most forward torso position. It is reported that Europeans of the time regarded the rumba as lewd and vulgar, the same way that Africans, in whose dances men and women rarely touched each other, felt about European couple dancing.

The three types of rumba represent the following:

In the *yambú*, the man chases the woman.

In the *guaguancó*, the man makes unanticipated pelvic thrusts or gestures from the Congo tradition while chasing the woman, who protects herself by hiding.

The **Columbia** was traditionally danced by men. In colonial times, there were more enslaved men than women, which resulted in men dancing together and creating a distinctive style. The quick, rhythmic foot patterns were frequently performed while elevated on the toes or balls of the feet. The lunging and vibrating seen in Abakuá dances are apparent. *Rumberos* have identified the rumba clave in Abakuá music.[11]

The Columbia was developed with a competitive purpose to its movements. Each man challenged another male dancer with a sequence of exceptional performances as he also competed with the skill of the *quinto* (soprano drum) player. The performances became dramatic rhythmic and movement exchanges; these exchanges included the performers being blindfolded using knives or instead dancing with glasses of water on their heads to exaggerate their competitive edge.

In recent years, a few older women have crossed the all-male frontier to compete with men in performing the Columbia. Now more young Cuban women perform the Columbia, and female international dance students are taught it. This provides teachers with an opportunity to obtain foreign currency, which is of more value than the Cuban peso.

Batárumba is a recent development combining the rumba with **Yoruba** batá drumming. On *Sabado de la rumba* (Rumba Saturday), the rumba is performed in public places by the national folkloric group.[12]

The rumba caught on in New York in the 1950s, then spread to Puerto Rico and elsewhere. By the 1950s, the recording, film, and broadcast industries had made Cuba the hub of Caribbean music. Cuban dance also reached a very high point in the 1950s, when the son, the mambo, and the cha-cha-chá were all popular. New York and Havana were the centers of the Latin dance craze.

MAMBO

Without the dance, the music will not live on.
        —Tito Puente, Cuban bandleader

The mambo originated in Cuba in large villages of Haitian immigrants. In Haiti, the "Mambo" is a voodoo priestess. Yet there is no dance in Haiti called the *mambo*. Mambo music was a fusion of Cuban music and swing. Bandleader Pérez Prado introduced this music in Havana in 1943 at the La Tropicana nightclub, and the mambo dance is attributed to him. Other Latin American band leaders, including Tito Puente, Tito Rodrígues, Pupi Campo, Machito, and Xavier Cugat, created their own styles, expanding the mambo craze. In Cuba, the foot pattern of the son (short, short, long) was changed to a touch step alternating from the right foot to the left. Touch right, step right, touch left, step left— the pelvis moving forward on each touch, step of the feet. The arms move forward and back in opposition to the feet. There is a bouncy up-and-down motion of the body with the occasional **shimmying** of the shoulders. Small turns and jumps and kicking patterns are added.[13]

CHA-CHA-CHÁ

In the early 1950s, band leader Enrique Jorrín introduced a medium-tempo rhythm that had a one, two, cha-cha-chá dance step. The cha-cha-chá rhythm was slower and easier to dance to than that of the mambo. Partners danced alternate parallel patterns moving in the same direction or in contrasting patterns moving toward or away from each other, in either closed or open position, while holding each other or separated. The cha-cha-chá became very popular in the United States, Europe, and Africa. The cha-cha-chá is danced competitively in the Latin categories of both American-style and international-style ballroom dance competitions.

THE EFFECT OF THE CUBAN REVOLUTION

The Cuban Revolution in 1959 significantly affected every aspect of Cuban life and culture. North Americans and Puerto Ricans were cut off from Cuban music and dance by the U.S. embargo. This started a rumor that communism had killed the arts in Cuba, whereas, in reality, since the 1970s, the communist government has given priority to arts and culture, especially music and dance.[14] While the outside world saw this era as a dark period for Cuban arts, the revolutionary leaders thought otherwise.

> Revolutionary leader Che Guevara envisioned Cuban communism not as a drab work regime but as a dynamic program of economic justice and lively popular culture—or, as he put it, as "socialism with pachanga" [referring to a popular dance rhythm of the 1950s].[15]

In the early 1990s, the loss of Soviet financial support, the hard-line communist policies, and the strengthened American embargo caused the collapse of the Cuban economy; yet the post-Soviet period was a productive time for dance and music. The contemporary **casino**-style salsa danced by couples was joined by the female-dominated **desperlote**, another salsa style, in which women shake freestyle with their hands in the air. The domination of this dance form by women reflects the independence and commercial direction of this money-driven environment. ***Casino de la rueda (salsa whelo)*** is a third form of the Cuban salsa, one in which couples dance intricate figures in a circle following the call of a leader.[16]

MAMBO IN THE UNITED STATES

Between 1947 and the early 1950s, the mambo craze obsessed the **mambonicks** in New York City. A toned-down version of mambo, without acrobatics and danced in the foot pattern of the son (short, short, long), was taught at dance studios, resort hotels, and nightclubs.

Mambo afforded members of diverse ethnicities, nationalities, and socio-economic backgrounds the opportunity to dance together. As Steven Loza said in *Creolizing Contradance in the Caribbean*, it was "the catalyst that brought Afro-Americans, Irish, Italians, Jews [together]. God, they danced that mambo. What social scientists couldn't do on purpose, the mambo was able to accomplish by error."[16]

The Palladium Ballroom on 53rd Street and Broadway in New York City, called the *Home of the Mambo*, was the laboratory for the Steven Loza quotation above. The Palladium no longer exists as a physical structure, but in order to maintain authenticity, the producers of the film *Mambo Kings* (1992) recreated the Palladium for the movie set. They also put Tito Puente on the bandstand and Pedro "Cuban Pete" Aguilar and Millie Donay on the dance floor. Cuban Pete was actually from Puerto Rico, but after band leader Ricky Ricardo introduced him as Cuban Pete, he kept the name. Cuban Pete taught Armand Assante and Antonio Banderas to dance for *Mambo Kings*. He and Millie Donay were the most famous mambo dancers of the time.

During the summers of the same period, the obsession with mambo spilled over to the resorts in the surrounding Catskill Mountains, where enthusiasts went to dance to the great Latin bands of the time. Featured performers included Machito, Tito Puente, and Tito Rodriguez. Hotels would often advertise their Latin band and dance team as their main attractions. Evening mambo shows were offered by even the smallest hotels.

The mambo, both inside and outside Cuba, began to feature partnering turns, which differentiated it from the typical sons from each zone of Cuba. Partners no longer were confined to dancing in closed positions—the woman was now led into complex turns under the man's upheld arm. It is now common in the international ballroom style of mambo for the couple to break the closed couple position and, reminiscent of dance with African styling, to move together but separated.

The mambo craze had only a short duration. Its tempo was altered, leading to the development of the cha-cha-chá. Eddie Torres, a New York dance teacher and choreographer, believes that the nightclub style of dancing mambo since the 1990s has become known as the salsa.

During the late 1940s to early 1950s, mambo became quite popular in New York City. The most famous performers of the time were the husband/wife dance team of Pedro "Cuban Pete" Aguilar and Millie Donay. Here, the couple performs at New York's Palladium ballroom in 1954.

In 1997, Ry Cooder produced the album (and Wim Wender produced the film) *The Buena Vista Social Club,* featuring octogenarian musicians performing nostalgic son and bolero from the 1920s. The film and readily available music led to a worldwide revival of interest in Cuban music, dance, and culture.

TRAINING CUBAN DANCERS

A rigorous dance training program is financed by the Cuban government. The program is based on the belief that everyone should, can, and does dance. Accessible dance training is available to the public as well as to both amateur and professional artists. Dancers are trained locally in folkloric, ballet, modern concert dance, and popular styles. Dancers with promise may audition for the provincial dance program, making them eligible to be placed in either the provincial or national art schools. The next level would be to audition for one of the few slots in the national dance training division. The final step is to audition for one of the six national dance companies: Danza Contemporánea de Cuba (modern concert dance), Conjunto Folklórico Nacional de Cuba (traditional folkloric forms), Ballet Nacional de Cuba (ballet company of Alicia Alonso), Ballet de Camagüey (ballet company of Fernando Alonso), Conjunto Folklórico de Oriente (traditional folkloric forms), and Ballet Folklórico Cutumba (traditional folkloric forms). Another option is extravaganza dance (theatrical presentations of primarily popular forms).[18]

Cuban dancers are afforded a wide range of nationally supported dance training opportunities in ballet, modern, and folkloric forms. These basic opportunities are not limited to those who seek careers in dance. Additional opportunities for advanced training are available to those talented individuals who desire to dance professionally. Cubans, therefore, are accomplished performers and teachers of dance and intelligent audience members and critics because of the multilevel opportunities to train in dance.

Dances of Hispaniola: Dominican Republic

In Santo Domingo, dance is the favorite passion; I think there is not another people in the world more fond of dance.

—Father Jean-Baptiste Labat, 1722[19]

Santo Domingo, as the Spanish half of Hispaniola was known, has an early colonial history resembling that of Cuba. The Spanish ruled the Caribbean island of Quisqueya, which they renamed Española (Hispaniola) from 1492, when Christopher Columbus arrived in the **West Indies**, so named because he believed he had reached the Indies in Asia. Spanish rule led to the eradication of the native **Ciboney Indian** and Taino Indian populations, despite the fact that the word *Taíno* meant "good" or "noble" in the Taino language, attributes that the Indians had showed Columbus and his Spanish crew with their peaceful and generous hospitality. The importation of enslaved Africans and the exhaustion of mineral reserves were followed by Spanish neglect

41

and malfeasance. The French conquest in 1795 interrupted Spanish control. In 1822, the independent Haitian government invaded Santo Domingo and occupied the region until 1844. Santo Domingo did not develop a plantation-based economy, and slavery did not play a major role in society.

Independence in 1844, when Santo Domingo became the Dominican Republic, failed to bring prosperity or stability. The country continued to be undeveloped and impoverished, and it was battered relentlessly by hurricanes. The U.S. Marine Corps' occupation of the country from 1916 to 1924 paved the way for the despot Rafael Trujillo to become dictator. This disordered history and unstable sovereignty led to a lack of ethnic or national identity.

The American occupation provoked guerilla resistance and inspired several nationalistic merengues such as Nico Lora's "La protesta," which is performed to this day. Dominicans came to resent U.S. rule and became caught up in a nationalistic fervor.[20]

The elite of **Cibao Valley**, who had previously avoided merengue for its vulgar lyrics, traded the **foxtrot** and danzón parties for salon adaptations of the local merengue. This movement led to the emergence of merengue as the national music and dance of the Dominican Republic.

MERENGUE TIPICO

Merengue is a product of creolization as most other mainstream Caribbean music and dance are. The origin of the word *merengue* is vague; it is believed to come from the Mozambican word *maringa*. A Haitian variation is documented in an 1822 reference to merengue's being danced for Haitian patrons.

This early ballroom merengue may have been mainly European in its foundation, but very different forms of merengue with a definite Afro-Cuban rhythm and call-and-response final section enjoyed great popularity outside the ballrooms. Traditional merengue differed from region to region. Merengue lyrics related many social topics, serving as a rich source of oral history. Many of the folk forms, which flourished in regional variations, were condemned as rude and offensive by the upper class, which preferred dainty waltzes, minuets, and foxtrots.[21]

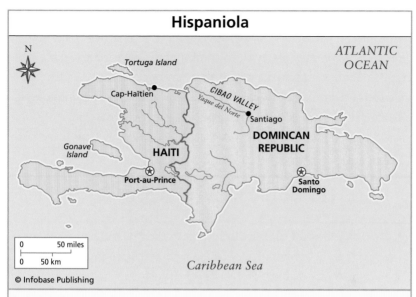

Hispaniola

N

ATLANTIC
OCEAN

Tortuga Island

Cap-Haïtien

CIBAO VALLEY
Yaque del Norte

Santiago

DOMINCAN
REPUBLIC

Gonave
Island

HAITI

Port-au-Prince

Santo
Domingo

0   50 miles

0   50 km

Caribbean Sea

© Infobase Publishing

The Island of Hispaniola is composed of the Caribbean nations
of the Dominican Republic and Haiti, both of which have a rich
dance tradition. Covering the eastern two-thirds of the island, the
Dominican Republic is the Caribbean's second-largest country,
behind Cuba.

Merengue of the heavily populated Cibao Valley became the most
significant form of the dance. A traditional merengue of the Cibao,
called the *merengue típico cibaeño*, had acquired a relatively standardized form by the 1930s. Numerous merengues typically began with a
brief paseo—a marchlike promenade, which couples performed by circling the floor. The second verse was called *merengue* and had topical
lyrics like the Cuban rumba and son. The next verse—a livelier section,
called **jaleo**—was an extended call-and-response section. This section
is now called mambo. The words *mambo, merengue, rumba, son,* and
tango sometimes occur arbitrarily, with or without a stylistic connection, in discussions of Caribbean dance and music.

Merengue típico cibaeño blossomed as folk entertainment in the
Cibao. It was performed at Sunday afternoon fiestas called **pasadias** and
at red-light bars in the provincial capital, Santiago de los Caballeros. The
"Ripped Parrot," the name of one of these bars, became an unofficial
nickname for the Cibao merengue.[22]

Merengue tipico differs from the contemporary son in its simpler harmonics, relentlessly quick tempo, and less complex choreography; it consists of a two-step pattern and continues to thrive in the Ciboa, especially in Santiago. Many have said that Santiago functions as the Nashville of the Dominican Republic. In recent years, the merengue típico cibaeño has continued to enjoy an impressive revitalization.

TRUJILLO: MUSIC AND DANCE

In 1930, Rafael Trujillo led a coup d'etat and seized the presidency, leading to a 31-year dictatorship that influenced every aspect of Dominican culture, including merengue. He discouraged international music such as jazz and rock 'n' roll. In conjunction with the Catholic Church, he restricted the Afro-Dominican religion and culture and recharged anti-Haitian phobias.

Trujillo grew up underprivileged and resented the elite who had barred him from their social clubs. He, therefore, promoted the Cibao-style merengue as a populist symbol and danced merengue at parties in his palaces. He took merengue groups on his campaigns and tours and commissioned hundreds of songs to sing the praises of his politics and activities. He insisted that urban dance bands play merengue as part of their performances.

Trujillo's brother, Petan, also a merengue lover, flooded radio and television broadcasts, which he controlled, with merengue music. By a 1936 decree, Trujillo declared a horn-based modernized version of Cibao merengue to be the national music and dance genre of the Dominican Republic. In 1961, Trujillo was assassinated. The most popular merengue at that time became "La muerte del chivo" (The Death of the Goat), written in celebration of his death.[23]

The national music and dance of the Dominican Republic, merengue is performed throughout the country. Here, a Dominican couple performs the dance in a local bar.

MODERN MERENGUE

The next chapter of Dominican history began after more political turbulence. Trujillo's right-hand man, Joaquín Balaguer, led a semidictatorship that lasted, with one eight-year interruption, through the late 1990s. The Balaguer regime was a continuation of the Trujillo regime without Trujillo because the Trujillo elite and the military remained in place. Yet in some ways, the Balaguer years established a new era for music and dance.

The dramatic urbanization of the country was stimulated by land acquisitions of multinational corporations. These acquisitions led to the uprooting of many thousands of farmers. These displaced persons flocked to urban shantytowns, many in Santo Domingo, the population of which doubled in the 1970s. A population that was 70 percent rural in the 1960s was now primarily urban.

Urbanization changed the country's population centers. The dramatic increase in foreign businesses, products, and media networks altered the course of popular music and dance in those growing cities. Merengue, which had previously monopolized the music scene, was now in competition with rock, pop, and salsa. These genres were backed by powerful multinationals, unlike in the Dominican recording industry under Petan Trujillo, which had discouraged competitors while producing few recordings. Merengue and other local music were, at first, at a disadvantage in competing with foreign music; however, the competition between local and foreign music led to the development of new sorts of national identity expressed in relation to the larger world. Reenergized by foreign influences that had formerly endangered it, merengue came to triumph in its homeland and overseas.

By the mid-1960s, rock music had made inroads into the Dominican music scene and has occupied a small niche ever since. The language barrier, anti-Americanism, and the love of Latin-style dancing saved the Dominican Republic from disco mania. **Balada**, or pop ballad, crooned by Marc Anthony, Julio Iglesias, and others, could be a relative of the bolero, a slow romantic Latin-American music and dance popular in the 1920s. The balada continues to compete with merengue and salsa on the airwaves but seldom as dance music.[24]

Salsa, which emerged in the 1960s as an expression of the New York City Latin experience and became an international spectacle, has had an essentially ambiguous role in Dominican culture. It is a vibrant pan-Latin music and dance that most Dominicans like, yet they regard it as foreign when compared with the indigenous merengue.

By 1980, the Dominican recording industry was prospering. Petan Trujillo was no longer in charge, and local record companies and studios were producing recordings that could hold their own against imports from abroad. **Salsa dura** had lost its freshness, and **salsa romantica,** which replaced it, was ordinary and commercial. The emergence of a new, rejuvenated merengue featured the sophistication of the big band merengue and the best influences from its foreign competitors.

By the early 1980s, merengue had triumphed in the Dominican Republic and spread to Puerto Rico and New York, where some **salsa** fans began to prefer merengue. The basic two-step merengue is easier to learn and to dance than is the salsa. Many who are intimidated by the more complicated salsa steps can easily dance to this Dominican beat. The merengue's basic step, called the *paso de la empalizada,* or the "stick-fence step," consists of stepping between the left and the right foot in time with the music. In both the salsa and the merengue, the choreography can include a variety of breaks, turns, and spins. Unlike movement in the salsa, embellishing turns in merengue can be done at a slow tempo. Many merengue dancers perform only the basic step.[25]

BACHATA

Bachata is a music and dance genre developed in the Dominican countryside in the 1960s. The name *bachata* was considered somewhat derogatory because of the poor inhabitants of the rural countryside where it originated. In the 1970s, the tempo was increased, and the lyrics became more vulgar. The offensive lyrics were another reason the name *bachata* was considered derogatory.

Unlike salsa, bachata does not follow the clave rhythm. It is often identified by a discordant guitar line and simple arrangements in 4/4 time. Bachata is a simple dance that is easy to learn. The basic step is a simple "one-two-three-hip." The following directions are for the leader:

JOHNNY VENTURA: LEGENDARY MERENGUERO "EL CABALLO"

Johnny Ventura, known as the legendary *merenguero* "El Caballo," was born in Santo Domingo on March 8, 1940. He was elected mayor of Santo Domingo in 1998. He began as a radio singer and later led his orchestra to enormous success. He is credited with defining popular Dominican music in the post-Trujillo age, for creating the sound of modern merengue, and for giving modern merengue its place in world music. He maintained some traditional aspects of merengue while enlivening it with foreign influences such as sophisticated salsa arrangements and the use of the bass drum from disco—these became standard features of merengue.

Inspired by James Brown, he dressed his orchestra in eye-catching costumes, and they performed stylish dance steps. The band embodied a new image of merengue as extravagant and glamorous, and, at the same time, indigenous. His work combined the best of local, international, traditional, and modern music.

Pictured here shortly after he was presented with a lifetime achievement award by the Latin Recording Academy in November 2006, Johnny Ventura is largely credited for creating the modern merengue sound in the Dominican Republic.

step side to left, side right, side left, and lift the right hip. The step then repeats itself but in reverse: step side to right, side left, side right, and lift the left hip. Then the step alternates, starting the sequence on the right and then on the left foot. Bachata is sometimes danced with a toe point on the fourth beat instead of a hip lift. Partners hold each other romantically and sway to the music. The fascinating hip (**Cuban hip motion**) and body motions enhance the simple steps. Some dancers pull their partners in close or execute turns to energize the dance.

In the 1990s, bachata changed dramatically. The tempo became faster with a bounce, shedding its resemblance to bolero. As with many popular dances, bachata lost its lower-class connotations and increased in mainstream popularity.[26]

Dances of Hispaniola: Haiti

The Spanish ruled the Caribbean island of Quisqueya, which they renamed Española (Hispaniola), from 1492 to 1697, when they ceded the western portion of the island to France. French colonists established sugarcane plantations and imported African slaves, who did the work of harvesting cane and processing it into molasses, sugar, and rum. The Haitian revolution (1791–1803) ended French rule. This left the government in the hands of the former *affranchi* class of freemen, composed of the *milat* (light-skinned freemen) and *nwa* (dark-skinned freemen), with the milat forming the more powerful elite group. Renamed "Haiti," an Arawak Indian name for "the land," the country has been self-governed since 1803, except for the years 1915 to 1934, when the United States occupied Haiti.

Unlike the Spanish-speaking countries of Latin America, including the Dominican Republic, which is also located on the island of Hispaniola, Haiti has its own distinct language, Haitian Creole (*Kreyòl ayisyen*). This language is predominantly French based and has incorporated vocabulary from African languages, Spanish, Portuguese, and English. Likewise, creolization of their religion, which incorporates Roman Catholicism and West African spirituality, produced vodou, which uses music and dance in its rituals honoring African spirits (*lwa*).

In Haiti, the celebration of Carnival demonstrates the joining of Catholic and West African spirituality. The festivities last for up to a week before Ash Wednesday. They feature revelers dancing in the streets and parades of highly decorated floats, elaborately dressed dance bands on flatbed trucks, and crowds of people moving through the streets to the rhythm of the music. Typically Haitian are the rara, street celebrations held each Sunday during Lent and in the week before Easter, in which musicians and dancers engage both in riotous behavior and in spiritual **vodou** ceremonies. Thinly veiled as part of the Christian celebration of Lent, these celebrations actually continue Carnival and celebrate the rebirth of spring. As Sloat observes, "In Haiti even many secular dances have roots in the spiritual tradition."[27] While most Haitian dance has its roots in vodou, some dances, including the affranchi *mereng*, are not considered to be associated with vodou, although ritual dances and Haitian secular folk dances influence each other.

Dance, an important element of street celebrations and religious devotion in Haiti, is also a social activity. European dance forms from the colonial period such as the contredanse, the quadrille, the waltz, and the polka underwent creolization in Haitian culture. The West African style dance that became the Haitian mereng, based on a five-note rhythm, evolved into a dance for the elite on the dance floor and a street dance for the working classes.

The American occupation of Haiti (1915–1934) brought with it the big band sound, jazz, and radio music. Although some welcomed these influences, many rejected them and stirred the population into a return to folk forms, especially the mereng. The call for a national Haitian music produced vodou-inspired musical compositions and the formation of folkloric dance companies.

The influence of Cuban son, Dominican merengue beats, and native Haitian *twoubadou* songs combined to form a creolized dance form of mereng, called **compas** (*konpa direk*) in the work of Nemours Jean-Baptiste in 1955. The compas has become the national dance of Haiti, a form for which it is now famous. The British invasion by The Beatles and other rock groups of the 1960s added rock to the Haitian repertoire of dance music. The elements of *vodou-djaz* (jazz), rap, and

In Haiti, rara bands entertain audiences during vodou ceremonies. Here, a rara group performs during the 2004 Smithsonian Folklife Festival in Washington, D.C.

raga also enjoy popularity in Haiti, yet the mereng (compas) remains the prominent dance form.

Even though mereng enjoys the primary place in Haitian social dance, by far the most extensive and influential dance forms are associated with vodou. According to Rol'hans Innocent, artistic director of Agoci Entertainment in Haiti, more than 100 African nations exist in Haitian vodou, each with its own form of dance. Dance in vodou tells ritualistic stories of encounters with the spirit world. These stories are centuries old and are handed down in song and movement from their West African origins. They form a cultural connection from past to present. Like other aspects of Haitian society, vodou has grown over the centuries, adding elements of Arawak Indian culture, French influences, and a dash of Roman Catholicism. The element of Roman Catholicism added respectability to vodou when the authorities, including the U.S. Marine Corps, which occupied Haiti in the early twentieth century, attempted to ban the African spirit worship.[28]

The movements of vodou dance reflect intentions: rapid rhythmic shoulder movement both clears the air and prepares for the reception of a spirit; flowing motions along the spinal column allow for relaxation and receptiveness to a spiritual mystery (possession); and the grinding of the hips is deliberately sexual in effect to expel a spirit. Vodou dances also had variations for special occasions such as initiation rites, family celebrations, and funerals, all of which connect human life with the spirit world.

Although these are among the chief dances of the vodou ceremonies and have also merged into the mainstream of twentieth-century Haitian folkloric dance, there are many more spiritual dances, rites, traditions, and variations from Africa that pervade Haitian spiritual dance. The creation of the folkloric movement in the 1940s is largely captured in Haiti in the work of Katherine Dunham. In 1943, the directors of education of the American Republics met in Panama and made recommendations about highlighting folkloric presentations by dance groups throughout the Americas. In Haiti, this work had already begun: Jacques Roumain had created the Bureau of Ethnology in 1941 and focused on Taino Indian and African music and dance in Haiti's development. The Bureau of Ethnology organized a troupe, *Mater Dolorosa*, to perform this music and dance. Music teacher Lina Blanchet took her Legba Singers to a Pan-American conference in Washington, D.C., during this period.

A political coup by Dumarsais Estimé in 1947 led to governmental approval of such groups as Haiti Chante et Danse and Troupe Macaya, both of which celebrated the African cultural legacy in Haiti. Eventually, under President Paul Eugene Magloire, some Haitian cultural leaders felt that a more refined technique was needed for the folkloric dance in Haiti. New York dancer and dance teacher Lavinia Williams, who had worked with Katherine Dunham, was recruited to go to Haiti, where she worked with the folkloric dancers from 1953 until her death in 1989.

A principal difficulty with staging a vodou dance as folklore, whether in Haiti or elsewhere, is its length, since the full ritual lasts for many hours, including the invocation of the principal deities in preliminary rites leading to the main ceremony. Creating a religious rite on a stage for

TYPICAL VODOU DANCES

According to Henry Frank, nearly all the Haitian ritual vodou dances have become secularized and form part of the social fabric of Haitian celebrations with no religious intent or meaning. They have also been the basis for many adaptations into the repertoire of folkloric dance groups in the United States and are common elements of black dance groups in America such as the groups formed by the pioneering Katherine Dunham and by the Alvin Ailey American Dance Theater. Typical vodou dances, described more fully by Frank, include the **yanvalou**, kongo, ibo, nago, djuba/martinique, petro, **banda**, and zarenyen. What follows is a short description of each dance.[29]

Yanvalou is a ritual dance from Benin that honors all the spirits of the Rada nation. Yanvalou represents the undulation of the waves in the water as they rise and fall and also the movement of the spirit, **Dambalah**, represented by a serpent. Dambalah is the source of energy and life. Since white is the color of the very pure Rada spirits, Agwe and Dambalah dancers wear white in the rites. A variation on the yanvalou is the **parigol,** a graceful and subtle dance associated with La Sirene, the mermaid.

Kongo, associated with the Congo nation, represents the beauty and majesty of the Haitian people. The Congo people are known for their sociability and gaiety. Dancers wear shiny, multicolored costumes.

Ibo represents the Ibo nation of Nigeria and expresses the pride of the Ibo people, who preferred death to

non-Haitian audience members, who may have little or no knowledge of what they are seeing, is yet another obstacle. In a traditional ceremony in Haiti, the entire assembly would know the melodies and lyrics and

enslavement. The movement of this dance is said to represent breaking the chains of slavery.

Nago derives from the Nagos of the interior of the former Slave Coast. This dance honors the spirits of power.
The dancers thrust their arms and chests forward, sug-
gesting that they are breaking through invisible barriers,
especially the chains of slavery.

Djuba/Martinique is a dance from the Djuba nation.
Blue is the color of the Djouba people, and the subtle swaying of the hips in Djouba shows the elegant flirtation between peasant men and women. **Kouzin** is the spirit honored in this dance. This dance is also related to the *zaka*, a
dance that depicts the hard labor of field work.

Petro has come to be associated with the Haitian revolution because a petro ritual in Bwa Cayiman preceded
the initial uprising in 1791. Petro is a fire dance that has
become a dance about sedition and change; the dancers
customarily wear red costumes.

Banda is a dance of the Guédé spirits, the spirits of the
life-and-death cycle. Guédé, the god of Death, is mocked in
the dance, which celebrates the passing of one human life
into its next stage—the germination into a new life. This
dance sometimes appears erotic, but it is meant as a celebration of new life more than exhibitionism. The Guédé
spirits wear black, white, and purple rags and sunglasses.
This dance belongs to the Rada rite.

Zarenyen is also a dance of the Guédé spirit family of
death. A person possessed by Guédé zarenyen moves in a
spiderlike fashion to a drumbeat different from the banda
tempo in this dance of the petro rite.

would sing them as a community. Another difficulty in recreating these
dances in the United States is the reputation vodou has as voodoo in
countless Hollywood movies that characterize the religious experience

In Haiti, ritual vodou dances are an important part of the social fabric of Haitian celebrations and can be both religious and secular. Here, women in Gonaïves, Haiti, partake in a vodou dance during Easter.

as a source of evil or humor. The association of voodoo with Satanism, zombies, and the undead is a stereotype that pervades popular culture from films to cartoons to video games. That depiction does great injustice to the vodou spiritual exercise and experience.

As a dynamic dance form, the secularized spiritual dance of the vodou rites continues to evolve, change, and add elements that keep it alive for the dancers and their audiences. Several companies have successfully recreated the Haitian vodou experience on the folkloric stages of the New York Haitian community, notably the Makandal company, and two more recent companies: Feet of Rhythm and Ti Ayiti. The common thread among Haitian dance companies in the United States is the presentation of Haitian culture as emphasizing beauty, precision in dance, and the joy that accompanies the religious experience in a community that celebrates itself.

Argentine Tango

Buenos Aires, Argentina, was founded by the Spanish in 1536, abandoned five years later, and founded again in 1580. In the 1870s, the **Araucanian Indians** still roamed the **Pampa**, which was also inhabited by the nomadic **gauchos**.

THE ORIGIN OF THE WORD *TANGO*

The origin of the word *tango* is not entirely clear. "Argentine historian Ricardo Rodriguez Molas . . . notes that in certain African tongues the word 'tango' means 'closed place' or reserved ground."[30] Another possibility is that it derives from Portuguese and thus from the Latin verb *tangere*, to touch, and was included in a type of **pidgin** Portuguese in connection with the slave trade. If this is correct, it was learned by African slaves from their captors. A third theory is that tango is a verbal expression of the sound of a drum beat: "tan-go".

TANGO DEFINED

The tango is man and woman in search of each other. It is the search for an embrace, a way to be together, when the man feels that he is a male and the woman feels that she is a female, without machismo. She likes to be led; he likes to lead. Disagreements may occur later or they may not. When that moment comes, it is important to have a positive and productive dialogue, fifty-fifty. The music arouses and torments, the dance is the coupling of two people defenseless against the world and powerless to change. This is the best definition of the tango as a dance, I think.

—Juan Carlos Copes, choreographer and dancer[31]

Dances are constantly changing, as are their names. In 1830, tango was not a specific dance but an event (as in "all-night tango") involving "any kind of dancing that black people did to drums."[32]

The term *tango americano* was sometimes given to the habanera, and the term *tango andaluz* was given a Spanish variation of the habanera. It is obvious that the word *tango* was recurring in the language of the late nineteenth-century population of Buenos Aires. It could easily be connected to any new dance form.

HABANERA

In 1816, the waltz came to Buenos Aires, and by mid-century, it was followed by the polka, the mazurka, and the schottische. In addition, the very popular habanera, also known as the andalusian tango, was imported during that period. The habanera evolved in Havana, Cuba, and migrated to Spain and Argentina. The habanera and the polka seem

Tango originated in Buenos Aires, Argentina, and Montevideo, Uruguay, around the mid-1850s and is danced throughout the world today. Here, a couple dances the tango in a Buenos Aires' café, while being accompanied by accordion music, though the dance is traditionally accompanied by a bandoneon.

to have stimulated the Argentine dance called the **milonga**, popular in the 1870s, with the *compadritos* of Buenos Aires and referred to as "the poor man's habanera."

MILONGA

Milonga began as a type of song. It was a modification of the long improvisations (accompanied by guitar) sung by the folk singers of the Pampa, the *payadores*. When the milonga reached Buenos Aires, the tempo was simplified, and steps were choreographed. There is not a specific description of the steps, but a strong inspiration from the newly imported habanera and polka are credited with milonga styling. The term *milonga* was also used to describe a place or an event where tango was danced.

The milonga, the maxixe, and the danzón were "dirty dances," dances in which partners held each other in close embrace. Those dances

COMPADRITOS AND THE CANDOMBE

Compadrito was an unflattering term used to describe mostly native-born poor young men seeking to imitate, in an exaggerated manner, the behavior and attitudes of the **compadres**. Their speech was Creole and traditional as opposed to immigrant based. They were street smart and dressed in the identifiable slouched grey hat, neckerchief (**lengue**), high-heeled boots, and knife.[33]

The early meaning of the word *tango* for a place where blacks came to dance played a part in the spontaneous conception of the Argentine tango. Most African Argentineans clustered in the inner city parishes where their culture, including their enthusiasm for dance festivals, had been preserved. Afro-Argentine dances differed from the dances of the Argentine villages or the European dances. The **candombe**, a blending of various African traditions, was the most significant dance. The complex choreography integrated a final section, blending wild rhythms, spontaneous steps, and energetic, powerful movements. Male candombe dancers showed their dance skills by using walking steps (**corridas**) and turns while flexing their knees. In the late 1870s, African Argentineans created a new dance, derived from the candombe, which they called the tango. The compadritos took parts of this dance and mockingly imitated them in their own favorite dance, the milonga, which eventually developed into the tango we know today.

crossed the lines of race and class and, in some cases, broke the law when members of different classes and races danced together. Dancers combined complex rhythms and pulsing hip actions as they danced to conventional music. These dances developed simultaneously in varied communities and soon became part of mixed-race gatherings.

The milonga, the maxixe, and the danzón each began as a spontaneous new way of dancing the existing dances. For this reason, they were very popular. Their African and European roots are intertwined. These dances thrived at carnival!

Corte y quebrada was the name given to the milonga dance technique. Cortes were the sudden turns and stops that cut the fluidity of the couple's movement as they crossed the floor. The corte was not a specific dance move but served as a prelude to the quebrada. Quebrada referred to the improvised, jerky swiveling hip motion—the more athletic and dramatic, the better. The novelty was that the cortes y quebradas were performed by dancers dancing together, not apart, as in the African-Argentinean tango.

The dance and music were refined by trial and error, the music being improvised by untrained musicians to fit the unpredictable movements created by the dancers. It seems quite evident that the milonga actually was the emerging structure of the tango before the new dance was named.

WEALTH AND IMMIGRATION

By 1879 General Julio Argentino Roca, who would later twice be president of Argentina, had cleared the Araucanian Indians from the Pampa, opening a vast area for ranching and farming. This action, coupled with an expanding market in Europe, led to the grandest economic expansion any Latin American country had ever experienced. By the 1920s, Argentina was one of the richest nations in the world and was seen as an immigration destination by millions of Europeans. One-half of these immigrants was from Italy, and one-third was from Spain. In a short period of time, the character of the Argentine people was drastically changed.

The wealthy patrician leaders of the republic planned to make their new federal capital the Paris of South America. The Barrio Norte, in the center of Buenos Aires, and the other northern barrios became the upper class area even as the barrios on the south side were populated by immigrants and those of the lower class. In the outer barrios, the old creole Argentina survived longer than it did in the city. The outer barrios were where the tango was born.

Male immigrants outnumbered females three to one. Women tango dancers were outnumbered approximately 10 to 1, which meant that only the best male dancers danced with a female partner. Male dancers reportedly often practiced tango with other male dancers until they reached a skill level enabling them to dance with women. The younger, inexperienced males danced the part of the woman. At times men with no partners used sticks or pool cues to simulate the legs of a woman as they practiced tango.

THE ITALIANIZATION OF THE TANGO

Over time, tango became popular in the dance halls patronized by Italian immigrants. These were more centrally located and hosted a poor, but more genteel, clientele. The rowdy and aggressive cortes y quebradas were subdued and **tango liso**, a smooth tango, developed. New instruments were added, and professional dancers worked in these clubs. Genuine dance academies opened, and smooth tango continued its evolution as the predecessor of the twentieth-century ballroom tango. At the same time, the intense fierceness of the tango steps that were preferred in the outer barrios faded. This gave rise to **lunfardo**, which is an expressive Italian-based language used by the writers of tango lyrics. Like tango, it became an integral part of the identity and culture of Buenos Aires.

Before 1900, dancers near the Rio de la Plata incorporated cortes into the interpretation of any international ballroom dance music. By the beginning of the twentieth century, tango had established itself in

Río de la Plata

This map shows the Rio de la Plata region of Buenos Aires, Argentina, and Montevideo, Uruguay, where tango originated.

Buenos Aires and in her sister city, Montevideo, Uruguay, across the Rio de la Plata.

Tango had become a popular dance by 1909. There were tango academies and dance halls. Women were dancing tango in public, yet they were not yet considered partners to the men; instead, they helped the men show off their tango flamboyance.

As the woman's role in tango became more equal, female tango dancers were still not considered "good girls" because the dancing was done late in the evening. Families allowed tango dancing in their homes in order to pass along steps from one family member to another, while continuing to disapprove of tango dance halls.

From the 1960s to the 1980s, tango declined in popularity as the youth of the Rio de la Plata region preferred Elvis Presley, The Beatles, and the Rolling Stones. Tango remained in the background at cafés but was no longer a significant part of popular culture until 1985. In 1983, the Argentine tango music and dance extravaganza *Tango Argentino* opened in Paris. In 1985, it played on and off Broadway to spellbound audiences. As the show traveled through Europe, Japan, and North America, captivated audiences were determined to learn the Argentine tango. In Buenos Aires, *Tango Argentino* led to a revitalized interest in tango. Young tango dancers began studying the dance from veteran dancers rather than learning it in the barrios.

In the mid-1990s, a growing number of Argentine tango instructors began touring the world, teaching the social way to dance tango. **Tangueros** were introduced to a way of dancing that was about the experience between a man and a woman. They embraced each other, dancing totally in the present, experiencing suggestion and response while moving around the floor expressing themselves through movement. Through workshops and travel to Argentina, North American tango

During the 1980s, tango experienced a resurgence in the Rio de la Plata region and it is today a hotbed for tango enthusiasts. Here, two professional tango dancers perform at the Galeria del Tango Argentino, one of Buenos Aires' famous bar-restaurants that offers nightly tango shows.

instructors have dramatically improved their skill. The world sees tango as a desirable commodity and tangueros flock to Buenos Aires to learn tango in its cultural setting.

THE DIFFERENCES BETWEEN ARGENTINE TANGO AND BALLROOM TANGO

Argentine tango, which is danced in both closed and open embrace, is based on improvisation. Speed and emotion are important factors when

TANGO BRANCHES OUT

The tango unexpectedly invaded dance floors in Paris and London in 1913 and 1914. These dancers, the same social elite respected by members of the upper class in Buenos Aries, began to put to rest their revulsion of tango. The tango arrived in Helsinki in 1913 and has become the national dance of Finland. In the winter of 1913 and 1914, tango reached New York. **Tangomania** then spread to Germany, Russia, and Italy. Japan has also become one of tango's strongholds. Shortly before this, in the late nineteenth century, the ***bandoneon*** was imported from Germany to replace organs in small village chapels. This cousin of the accordion became the characteristic tango instrument.

In the early twentieth century, tango was banned by the Pope after a private viewing. Kaiser Wilhelm I did not allow his officers to dance tango when wearing their uniforms. This ruling banned tango from being danced at all state balls because the officers would be in uniform.

The *tango a la francesa*—the tango that Paris sent back to Argentina after 1913—returned in a much tamer form performing the dance. It continues to evolve in Argentina and the many other large tango centers around the world. Instructors do, however, use step patterns and sequences of steps when teaching the dance to novices. Yet the ultimate goal is to learn to dance in the moment while spontaneously interpreting the music.

Ballroom tango steps have been standardized and codified by dance studios and professional dance organizations in their syllabi. American style tango, which is danced in both closed and open positions, is structured to musical phrasing. International style tango is danced only in closed embrace. In DanceSport competitions, tango is danced in international style standard competitions and also American style smooth competitions.

than when it left. In September 1913, Baron Antonio de Marchi organized a three-day tango festival at the Palace Theatre in Corrientes Street, sponsored by a committee of ladies of impeccable upper-class breeding. In the years after this festival, tango was openly danced in middle-class households and mansions of the Barrio Norte in Buenos Aires.

By the 1930s, tango was out of date in Paris but was entering its golden age in Argentina. During the 1940s, the third and final decade of the "golden age," tango was at the height of its popularity. The clubs were overcrowded with dancers, and orchestras had to be booked a year in advance to insure that there would be music for dance parties. At Carnival time, dances were held in every available venue. When the dance halls were all filled, dances were scheduled in athletic arenas and stadiums. These venues were so crowded that dancers were compelled to take smaller and smaller steps. So many dancers were crowded into each space that the style of dancing tango had to change. In the 1950s, the golden age of tango drew to a close.

RUDOLPH VALENTINO AND TANGO IN FILM

In Hollywood films of the 1920s, the tango illustrated the fantasy of the "Latin Lover." Rudolph Valentino arrived in New York from Italy in 1913 and, after several menial jobs, began dancing in nightclubs and dance halls. *The Four Horsemen of the Apocalypse*, a film in which he danced the tango in both the Hollywood gaucho and Parisian styles, made him a star. He also danced the tango in *Blood and Sand* in 1922. In the 1977 film *Valentino*, a story about his life, Rudolph Nureyev portrayed Valentino. In this film, he taught the tango to **Vaslav Nijinsky**, portrayed by Anthony Dowell. What follows is a list of some of the movies that have featured tango, followed by the actors/actresses who danced the tango:

1917   *El Tango de la Muerte*—Nelo Cosimi, Pascual Demarco, and Manuel Lamas

1921   *The Four Horsemen of the Apocalypse*— Rudolph Valentino

1922   *Blood and Sand*—Rudolph Valentino

1933   *Flying Down to Rio*—Fred Astaire, Ginger Rogers, and Dolores del Rio
Tango!—El Cachafaz

1934   *El Tango en Broadway*—Carlos Gardel, Vincente Padula, and Trini Ramos

1935   *El Día Que Me Quieras*—Carlos Gardel and Rosita Moreno
Go Into Your Dance—Ruby Keeler

Tango Bar—Carlos Gardel, Enrique de Rosas, Tito Lusiardo, and Rosita Moreno

1940   *Down Argentine Way*—Betty Grable

1950   *Sunset Boulevard*—William Holden and Gloria Swanson

1972   *Last Tango in Paris*—Marlon Brando and Maria Schneider

1977   *Valentino*—Rudolf Nureyev and Anthony Dowell

1984   *The Cotton Club*—Richard Gere

1992   *Scent of a Woman*—Al Pachino and Gabrielle Anwar

Indochine—Catherine Deneuve and Linh Dan Pham

1994   *True Lies* —Tia Carrere, Jamie Lee Curtis, and Arnold Schwarzenegger

1998   *Tango*—Sandra Ballesteros

2001   *Moulin Rouge*—Two minor characters perform a tango.

2002   *The Tuxedo*—Jackie Chan used a dance-double for his tango scene.

2003   *Assassination Tango*—Robert Duvall and Luciana Pedraza

2004   *Shall We Dance?*—Richard Gere and Jennifer Lopez

2006   *Take the Lead*—Antonio Banderas and Katya Virshilas

2008   *Another Cinderella Story*—Selena Gomez and Andrew Seeley

Café de Los Maestros—Argentinian tango documentary

6

Dance of Brazil: Samba

THE ROOTS OF SAMBA

Brazil, the largest of the South American countries, is world famous for its Carnival preceding Lent each year. It is also world famous for its national dance, the samba.

Brazil was discovered by the Portuguese in the European search for a trade route to the Far East. The Treaty of Tordesillas (1494), signed by the Spanish monarchs of Castile and Aragon as well as Portugal, gave Portugal possession of this and other lands. The impetus for finding a sea route to the East was both commercial and religious; Europeans had no desire to pay tolls and fees to those who controlled the land route to the East along the Silk Road, especially because that meant paying monetary tribute to the Muslim rulers of those lands. Although adjustments were made to the demarcation line the treaty set forth—with Spain claiming lands west of the line and Portugal claiming lands east of the line—the Spanish did not oppose the Portuguese expansion into more of what would become Brazil.

Like other European colonists, the Portuguese imported ever-increasing numbers of Africans who were sold into slavery along the

West Coast of Africa and transported to the New World. They worked for the colonists, whose goal was principally to send resources back to Portugal. The estimated number of enslaved Africans in colonial Brazil and in the independent republic, up until 1888, was in the millions. The main export from Brazil in the early decades of colonization was brazilwood, for which the country was named. Eventually, sugarcane plantations increased the demand for more workers, especially enslaved Africans. Although many slaves escaped into the interior of Brazil, they were eventually recaptured or killed. More commonly, slaves intermarried with the Portuguese colonists so that, long before the abolition of slavery in 1888, large numbers of slaves had merged with the European Portuguese population. The population center for sugarcane plantations was in the northeastern part of the country. The site of the future city of Rio de Janeiro was discovered in 1502. Rio de Janeiro was the capital of Brazil from1763 to 1960, including the colonial period through Brazil's birth as an independent nation in 1822 until the new city of Brasilia became the capital in 1960. This history set the stage for the birth of the samba there.

THE MAXIXE

The maxixe, known as the Brazilian tango, is an Afro-Brazilian dance developed by slaves from Mozambique in Rio de Janeiro in the 1860s, just as tango was developing in Argentina. It features a fast 2/4 rhythm and is danced with a bent posture. The maxixe was first documented in 1883 and, by the 1890s, had become the primary carnival dance in Rio de Janeiro.

In 1919, maxixe was the most popular dance of urban Brazil. Maxixe was identified with the *Cidade Nova*, or "new city," of Rio de Janerio. It articulated an African influence in Brazilian music and dance.[34] In the 1920s, maxixe was forbidden in Brazil because of the intertwining of the man and the woman as they danced.

Maxixe became popular in Europe, North America, and several South American countries, including Argentina and Uruguay, in the first decades of the twentieth century. It was a forerunner of the samba.

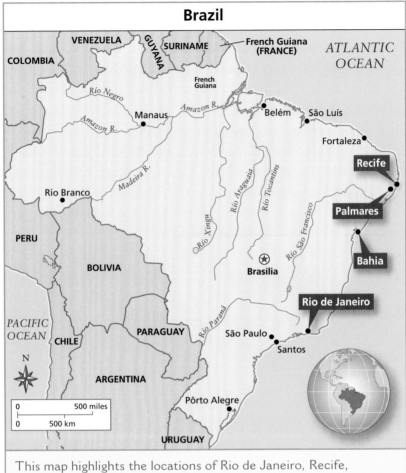

Brazil

This map highlights the locations of Rio de Janeiro, Recife, Palmares, and Bahia, Brazil. Each of these cities has played a leading role in the development of Brazilian dance.

THE BIRTH OF THE SAMBA

The samba is a joyful Afro-Brazilian dance that originated in the late nineteenth century in Rio de Janeiro and was derived from a West African dance called the **lundu**. It evolved into the **zemba queca** by 1885 and became known as the samba when it was mixed with the maxixe in the early twentieth century. Samba seemed perfectly made for the Carnival parades that originated in Rio de Janeiro about the middle of the nineteenth century and soon became a staple of the festival.

THE SAMBA SCHOOLS
AND THE SAMBADROME

The formation of samba schools in 1928, like the formation of **capoeira** schools in 1932, became part of a concerted effort to forge a national identity in Brazil.[35] The formation of a national identity came at a time when the leaders of Brazil wanted to celebrate its unity through diversity. The samba schools participate in Rio de Janeiro's Carnival held each year, but they do much more than that: they also serve as neighborhood social gathering places and social service agencies. Carnival is considered by many to be an outlet from the frustrations of daily life, a time of release and relaxation from the daily cares of urban life. The Sambadrome was built to house the samba parade in 1984 after more than a century of growth of the Carnival had made the event unwieldy, with bleachers erected just before the event and then removed as soon as the parade ended. This "Stadium of Samba" is a self-contained series of concrete buildings with an open-air segment (Samba Runway) and other sections open, or covered, for seating and standing while viewing the parade.

SAMBA AND ITS VARIATIONS

Called by Barbara Browning "the dance of the body articulate,"[36] the music of the samba has a 2/4 rhythm. The dance itself has three steps to every bar, making it feel like a dance in 3/4 time, the same as waltz time, with a feel of a step-ball-change dance movement. Throughout her analyses of Brazilian dances, Browning makes the more than valid point that "the boundaries between specific dance forms seem to disintegrate . . . gestures from religious and martial dance resonate in the secular samba—and samba infiltrates the circles of **candomblé** (African religion) and capoeira."[37]

Samba no pé is a solo dance that is the characteristic dance of the Carnival parades. The basic movement involves an upright posture, bending one knee at a time. The dance follows the beat of the music and can go from an average pace to very fast. Men dance with the whole foot

Built in 1984, Rio de Janeiro's Sambadrome is a permanent parade ground that stretches nearly half a mile and has seating for 90,000 spectators. Here, the Portela samba school dances its way down an open portion of the Sambadrome during Carnival in February 2009.

on the ground while women, usually in high heels, dance on the balls of the feet. Even though this is the most popular form of samba, there are regional variations, usually dependent upon the music of the region.

Samba axé is a solo samba that dates from the early 1990s in the northeastern province of Bahia when the axé rhythm replaced the more usual **lambada** rhythm. This high-energy, fast-paced dance does not retain the basics of samba no pé but is more improvisational as it adds more athleticism to the dancers' movements. **Samba reggae** adds the reggae drumbeat to the traditional samba music; it is also from Bahia but is danced throughout Brazil.

Brazilian ballroom samba, or *samba de gafieira*, is a partner dance but is quite unlike international ballroom samba. It appeared in the 1940s and takes its name from the *gafieira*—popular urban nightclubs of Rio de Janeiro at that time. Evolved from the maxixe, it has some entwined leg movements of the Argentine tango and sometimes resembles an acrobatic waltz. Samba de gafieira has incorporated many acrobatic movements and has evolved to become the most complex dancing style of samba in Brazil. **Cocktail samba** is a variant of this dance form. **Samba rock** is a Latin nightclub partner dance that started in São Paulo and resembles a mix of Brazilian ballroom samba de gafieira and salsa. *Samba pagode* is a partner dance that resembles the samba de gafieira but is more subdued and intimate.

Samba de roda is performed by many capoeira groups as a traditional Afro-Brazilian dance that accompanies the ceremonial aspects of a capoeira game. It originated in Bahia in northern Brazil among West African slaves, many of whom immigrated to the then capital of Brazil, Rio de Janeiro, spreading its popularity throughout the southern states of the country. In 2005, the United Nations Educational, Scientific, and Cultural Organization (UNESCO) named the Bahian samba de roda a "Heritage of Humanity."

Lambada evolved from the samba, the **carimbó**, and other Latin dances in the 1980s. Both the carimbo and the lambada are sensual Brazilian couple dances in which the woman twists and turns. Lambada, like many Latin dances, has an obscure meaning but could refer to a whiplike motion. The dancers reproduce this whiplike or wavelike motion by swaying. The lambada enjoyed a brief popularity in northern Brazil. It began as a two-beat dance similar to the merengue and became

The samba has many variations, including samba de roda, samba de gafieira, samba axé, and samba no pé. Here, members of the Viradouro Samba School perform during Carnival in Rio de Janeiro in February 2009.

a four-beat dance when new music was composed for it. The motion of the lambada is side to side and not front to back. In 1989, a French entrepreneur, Olivier Lamotte d'Incamps, began a publicity campaign to popularize the lambada in Europe and then worldwide; it remained popular in Japan for many years after a brief craze swept Europe and North America. The lambada is closely linked to the maxixe, a dance that was forbidden in Brazil in the 1920s because of the way the man and woman intertwined their bodies in the dance. Identifying the lambada as a forbidden dance fueled its short-lived popularity.

The **bossa nova** was an earlier dance craze from the 1960s that had several variations, one of which resembled the samba step, danced with soft knees that allow for sideways motion and swinging hips. Like the music that prompted it, and despite heavy publicity, the bossa nova vanished soon after its appearance.

International ballroom samba differs from other forms of samba and has several levels of teaching syllabi sanctioned by the International Dance Teachers Association and the Imperial Society of Teachers of Dancing. Samba has also become part of the video-exercise industry in which dancers perform the samba as a means of exercise with the object of weight loss and muscle toning through dancing. Samba reggae, a variation that gained rapid acceptance in the exercise world of the early twenty-first century, is in this category.

Dance of Brazil: Capoeira

ROOTS OF THE CAPOEIRA

In the Portuguese colony of Brazil, following its European discovery, millions of Black Africans were sold into slavery and shipped to the New World to work for their European masters, first cutting brazilwood trees for export and then working in the expanding sugarcane plantations of northeastern Brazil.

The capoeira evolved as an Afro-Brazilian art form that combines martial arts, music, dance, and games. Those who play the capoeira are called **capoeiras** (singular: capoeirista). The origin of capoeira is obscure, some arguing that it arose in Africa and was brought to the New World by African slaves, others claiming that it is a Brazilian art form created by groups of escaped slaves for defensive purposes. According to one theory, in the early seventeenth century in Recife, a group of 40 slaves rebelled against their master, killed all the white employees, and burned the plantation. They headed to the mountains, where they founded Palmares, an African community that lasted nearly a century and grew to more than 20,000 people—black, white, and Indian. It is thought that Palmares is where the first forms of capoeira were developed. Whatever

78

Introduced by slaves sometime after the sixteenth century, capoeira is an Afro-Brazilian art form that combines martial arts, music, dance, and games. Here, a couple of capoeira dancers perform on the streets of Olinda, Brazil.

its true origin, capoeira was first developed by slaves from West Africa, mainly from present-day Angola. It is a mixture of Congolese and Yoruban culture with a nod to the dominant Roman Catholic culture of the Brazilian elite, who determined social policies and customs.

One theory holds that it was originally a form of martial art that had to be disguised by the slaves as a game of singing and dancing so that their masters would not suspect their training. Certainly the police records from nineteenth-century Brazil illustrate that capoeira was a punishable offense, most often carried out by flogging. The association of this form of street fighting with criminal activity has a long history, and it became a severe social problem immediately after the abolition of slavery in Brazil in 1888. With little prospect of finding employment and with deplorable living conditions in the shantytowns of Rio de Janeiro, growing numbers of street gangs harassed and robbed more affluent citizens by using capoeira aggressively. Capoeira was finally outlawed in 1890. Criminalizing the practice only served to send it underground. Street fighters took on nicknames to conceal their identities and became craftier at evading police. They were more cautious about approaching their potential victims and more secretive in passing on their art to the succeeding generation. Still practiced in the poorer sections of Rio de Janeiro, its suppression has resulted in riots that some allege the police provoked.

In the 1890s, some people in high levels of society practiced capoeira. In response, the president created a special police force to control the situation, and a tougher law was later added, stating that any person who was a known capoeirista would be expatriated. To enforce these laws, the president named Joao Batista Sampaio Ferraz, an excellent capoeirista himself and reputed to be the most ruthless police chief in Brazil's history, determined to stamp out capoeira. Sampaio's special police force learned capoeira and arrested a capoeirista named Juca Reis, a member of Rio de Janeiro's elite class, and demanded that he be deported. Members of the president's cabinet opposed this action because Reis's father was well known and favored by many politicians. The president called a special meeting of his cabinet; after 18 days of meeting, two cabinet members resigned, and Reis was, in fact, deported. The opposition to this unpopular government created a black militia to disrupt the president and his cabinet. This militia, formed exclusively of capoeiras, spread fear in the capital. The police could not contain them; just as the situation became alarming, Brazil went to war with Paraguay. The black militia went to the front and became heroes, thus changing the fortune of the capoeira.

In the early twentieth century, the Brazilian capoeira became recognized both as a martial art and as a national sport as Brazil's government sought to forge a national identity. Mestre Bimba (Manuel dos Reis Machado) founded the first capoeira school in 1932 and created the capoeira regional style, which differed from the traditional capoeira Angola. Mestre Bimba is called the father of modern capoeira. According to Talmon-Chvaicer (2008), in the 1930s, scholars such as Gilberto Freyre and others began to value the influence of African and indigenous Indian cultures on the Brazilian identity. By the late 1930s, an

THE DANCE/JOGO

The game (*jogo*) or dance of Capoeira is played in a circle (**roda**) with songs and musical accompaniment, usually a drum, a bell, stringed instruments, tambourines, a double gong, a rasp, and stringed bows called **berimbaus**. Because the circle encloses the fighters (dancers), those not in the circle cannot see what happens within it. This formation was a definite plus in the days when the dance was outlawed because it gave the fighters time to react to a potential intrusion and time for the circle to dissolve. The musicians form a **bateria** at the head, or "mouth," of the circle, and participants enter the circle in front of the musicians. The speed of this gamelike dance depends upon the tempo of the musicians. The game has three sorts of songs. It opens with a **ladainha**, a litanylike song followed by other call-and-response songs (**chula** or **louvação**) and a series of songs (**corridos**) sung during the game. One type of music for the dance is the samba de roda.

The players join the onlookers in the circumference of the circle and enter the center of the circle in pairs for the battle dance. This dance is characterized by lithe, fluid movements; feints and parries; evasive techniques and handstands; kicks, sweeps, and head butts; and cartwheels and rolls. The object is not to injure an opponent but to show skill in delivering near blows and, more to the point, in evading them. Cunning and stealth are principal goals of the game, and it involves participants becoming superior at trickery or deceit, called **malicia**, which tricks one's opponent into committing to an action that leaves him or her open to a full-fledged blow. As students develop a repertoire of moves and feints, sharpen their observational skills, and anticipate the moves and feints of their opponents, they begin to perfect their art of trickery, or **malandragem**.

inclusive emphasis on the Brazilian national identity came to prize the contributions of blacks, Indians, whites, and **mestizos** to a unified Brazil, where all could live in harmony without racial strife. The president, Getúlio Vargas (1937–1945), inaugurated the new state policy. The newly formed capoeira schools were ready to take their places as part of the new national identity, along with the recently formed samba schools.

Within a capoeira performance, one element may be the samba da roda, a traditional Afro-Brazilian dance. Allegedly, during the periods in which capoeira was banned, the dance elements were emphasized, disguising the sometimes lethal street fighting of the nineteenth

DANCEBRAZIL

DanceBrazil, which Jelon Vieira established in New York City in 1977, has led to an understanding and appreciation for capoeira in the United States. In 1980, Alvin Ailey joined the board of directors of DanceBrazil and guided the organization toward future success. Soon DanceBrazil was featured at Lincoln Center, and Ailey and the board premiered *Orfeo Negro* in 1985 at the Riverside Dance Festival. DanceBrazil has been thrilling and educating audiences for more than 30 years.

In September 2008, Artistic Director Jelon Vieira was awarded one of only 11 National Heritage Fellowships, the country's highest honor in the folk and traditional arts conferred by the National Endowment for the Arts in Washington, D.C. Mr. Vieira teaches capoeira in both Brazil and the United States. Notable students include soccer great Pelé and film stars Wesley Snipes and Eddie Murphy. A long-term goal of Mr. Vieira is to establish a capoeira center for underprivileged children in Brazil. He believes that by using capoeira to build self-esteem and self-discipline, it may be possible to move these children from the streets and into the educational system and society.

century. The varied dance styles associated with earlier forms of capoeira served to draw attention away from the illegal combat. In modern capoeira, dance remains an important element, beginning with
a back and forth swaying (**ginga**). The feet are kept a shoulder width
apart and rock back and forth in a triangular movement. The arms
are involved to parry potential thrusts, and the torso moves back and
forth in either a defensive or offensive position. As the players warm
up, the more combative elements of the form begin to appear as two
dancers (opponents) face each other. The attacks involve kicks, sweeps,
and head butts. Occasionally, hand strikes may occur, but they are not

In 1977, Brazilian choreographer Jelon Vieira brought
capoeira to New York City in the form of DanceBrazil.
Here, members of Dance Brazil perform during Vieira's
Camara at the Joyce Theater.

favored. The feet, in the West African form of dance, were thought by some to be used for destroying; others contend that the hands of slaves were often shackled and could not be used for striking. Elbow strikes are more common. The evasive techniques mentioned above complement the feints and thrusts of the attacker. In the jogo, however, the attacks do not usually come to completion, and blows do not land. The most skillful of the players will show the most cunning and put his or her opponent at the most risk of attack.

Sometimes the game will begin with, or be interrupted by, a *chamada* in which one player calls another to the circle. This signals an approach that can be filled with danger and must be made warily as the caller and the responder promenade closely together inside the circle. The more proficient player points out to the less proficient player the opportunities that could have been used to strike. This technique is one of the ways in which the masters and professors teach those new to the game.

In modern capoeira, capoeiras have different rankings from student through master with degrees of proficiency in between, much like the different degrees in the eastern martial arts. Students are given their first ranking at their "baptism," a ceremony that recalls the taking of a nickname in former times and that may include taking a new name. The masters (*mestres*) are the spokesmen of capoeira and usually head up their own schools. Dances similar to capoeira, called **danymé** or **ladjá**, are practiced in Martinique. In Cuba, a mock battle dance called **maní** uses moves similar to those of capoeira and also some tactics from *samba duro*, which originated in El Salvador.

Immigrants from Brazil have maintained the traditional teachings of capoeira and have established more than 500 schools in the United States, considerably more than in Brazil. There is currently a minimum of one Capoeira school in each of the 50 states. Capoeira is taught in schools of dance throughout the world. There are schools on every continent except Antarctica.

Salsa

THE ROOTS OF SALSA

The mambo, at its peak in New York City in the 1950s, set the stage for the salsa boom of the 1970s. In the 1950s, Arsenio Rodriguez moved from Cuba to New York, where he laid the foundations for salsa, a dance that was taking the Latin music scene by storm.[38]

The term *salsa dance* was created in New York in the 1960s, but salsa's dance moves developed from a centuries-old Latin dance tradition. Each new music and dance genre needs a catchy commercial title. This new dance—called salsa, which means "hot sauce"—was used to describe the combination of son, the mambo, and the rumba, which had become the modern Cuban dance music.[39] The term *salsa*, defining danceable Latin music, was coined in 1933, when Ignacio Piñeiro, a Cuban composer, wrote the song "Échale Salsita." Alfredo Valdés Sr. related that the idea occurred to Piñerio after eating food with no Cuban spices—it would serve as a type of protest against bland food. Salsa became a popular nickname for a variety of Latin and Afro-Caribbean music, some of which are the rumba, the son, the mambo, the cha-cha-chá, the merengue, the **cumbia,** and others. These different sounds continued to be mixed and fused. Commercial salsa music was being produced in greater volume because of the increased investment in, and promotion of, salsa. In the 1960s, the name salsa became popular. An early salsa album, Cal Tjader Quintet plus 5's *Cal Tjader Soul Sauce,* featured a plate of red beans and chili with a fork and an opened bottle of Tabasco sauce on the cover. Tjader's style of music was called salsa by many Mexicans in San Francisco. His music spread to other markets, including Los Angeles and the East Coast, leading to Latin music being aired on radio stations across the country. Salsa again materialized in the late 1960s as a Cuban-style music played primarily by Puerto Ricans to express the New York City Latin experience.[40] This modern dance variation on son developed outside Cuba.

Salsa evolved as a distillation of many Latin and Afro-Caribbean dances. A large part of the dance originated in Cuba, where the French, who fled from Haiti in the late eighteenth century, brought the danzón and other country dances from England and France. These dances were mixed with the African rumbas. Added to this was the Cuban son. This manner of fusing diverse music and dance forms also occurred elsewhere in Latin America and the Caribbean, including Puerto Rico and Colombia.

FANIA RECORDS

In 1964, Johnny Pacheco, a band leader with Dominican parents who liked Cuban music, established Fania Records, an independent label. Pacheco distributed records produced by Fania Records to local stores out of the trunk of his car. In 1967, Fania Records came under the management of Jerry Masucci, who launched an aggressive and very successful program of recording and promoting musicians. Early performers of Fania Records included boogaloo king Ray Barretto and Johnny Pacheco, whose sound in the 1970s was defined by the barrio-based groups they recruited and promoted.

A decade later, in 1974, Fania Records released Larry Harlow's *Salsa;* it sold many copies, making him a celebrity and popularizing the name salsa. At this time, most Afro-Cuban rhythms, and what was thought to be exciting in Latin music, were called salsa. "Salsa Explosion," a

The term *salsa* was coined in 1933 by Cuban composer Ignacio Piñeiro, but the dance didn't become a sensation until the 1960s, when a number of Latino groups made it popular on the East Coast. Here, actress Cloris Leachman and professional dancer Corky Ballas dance the salsa on ABC's *Dancing with the Stars* in 2008.

24-page insert in the June 1976 issue of *Billboard*, was dedicated to Latin music. At this time salsa also gained attention in the Anglo market.

Salsero Sergio George describes salsa of the late 1960s and early 1970s: "In my opinion, the true salsa sound of that era was the musical fusion of New York with Puerto Rico, with Cuba and with Africa; that whole fusion was for me the true roots of salsa in the late '60s, early '70s. It came out of a street sound. People jamming in the park with the congas and somebody coming to sing . . . . That was the raw street salsa sound."[41]

The great Puerto Rican migration to the United States began when residents of the island were granted U.S. citizenship in 1917. Immigrating Puerto Ricans in very large proportion preserved their identity by maintaining their language, food, and music. In the 1950s, more than half a million Puerto Ricans migrated.

The popular Latin music of New York has complex layers blending Cuban, Puerto Rican, and other Latin American beats with jazz, rock, and soul. This progression of music and dance blending, which began in the 1930s and continued for 40 years until the 1970s, became the New York–Caribbean dance phenomenon known as salsa.

The salsa lyrics relate stories of displacement, survival, and hope. Puerto Rican salsa is composed on a three-two clave, "one, two, three—one, two," over which melodic variations and polyrhythms are layered. Salsa changes with the locale and from one song to the next. Dancers enjoy the variety and complexity of the music.

Salsa can be danced on different notes, but it is important to step in time to the rhythm. Salsa music, lyrics, and steps combine to form an intricately syncopated whole. Dancers are free to move and respond to the music. The sensual pelvic movements and quick, complicated foot patterns are exciting. Salsa's sexuality, partnering, and performance quality lead to a climax in intensity reminiscent of a cleansing and renewal ritual.

To attend a Latin dance club in New York, Miami, Havana, or San Juan is to see several hundred dancers in motion. Salsa is a stylish and sophisticated couple's dance totally different from the formless shuffling often seen accompanying American pop music. The basic foot patterns and resulting hip action may be somewhat uniform, but skilled salsa dancers combine the steps with amazing variety. The male partner leads the female in numerous turns and spins that create a flashy dance performance.

Latin dance clubs differ from rock clubs and other American dance scenes. The purpose of attending a salsa club is to dance—not to watch. Dancers from 20-year-olds to 80-year-olds, and even older, enjoy this dance. In some instances, the older dancers will be the better dancers. There is little need for the youth to develop their own counter-culture dance and music when a dance genre as rich as this has been a part of the culture for so long.

Whites, blacks, mulattos, and Asians mingle together while dancing salsa with acceptance and openness, reflecting the racial synthesis that originally produced Cuban dance music.[42]

CONTEMPORARY CUBAN SALSA

Casino Salsa

Casino salsa is danced only by couples. Nonstop turning figures are the signature movements of casino-style salsa. The man leads the woman into numerous turns by lifting his arms. Casino dancers spin

"ON TWO" DANCERS: SHINES

Since the 1990s, in New York and to a lesser extent on the international salsa scene, the "on two" dancers formed a subculture of salsa dancers who preferred to dance salsa "on two," taking the first step of the four-beat foot pattern on the second beat rather than the first beat as is done in traditional salsa dancing. Dance steps or sequences performed to the beat of the clave, dancing apart from one's partner, are called **shines**. Traditionally, the man would begin (right-pause-left-right/left-pause-right-left). "On two" dancers prefer a flashier style with fancy footwork, known as "shines," and complex turns. These dancers, many from New York City and others mostly from the middle class, learn and develop their moves at commercial dance studios, at salsa exhibitions by dance companies, at the large salsa congresses, and informally at salsa clubs.

Any step done apart from a partner is an example of a shine. Shines are usually danced by following the leader with your partner or by competitively trading "shines" in a face-off with your partner. Eddie Torres, a New York dance teacher and choreographer, lists a vast array of different shines on his Web site with a breakdown in clave timing for both men and women. He believes that the salsa is the nightclub style of dancing the mambo. Some have called traditional salsa "Mambo on the One."

In recent years, Latin dance clubs have become popular in such cities as New York, Miami, Havana, and San Juan. Here, a couple of salsa dancers perform at one of Manhattan's salsa clubs.

around in relation to one another while maintaining contact with one or both hands and frequently looping their arms into a "pretzel" and out again.

Casino de la Rueda (Salsa in the Round)

Casino de la rueda is a contemporary form of Cuban-style salsa in which a group of couples dance combinations of steps in a circle following a leader. It is usually danced by four couples, who alternate dancing with their original partner, facing partners, and **corners**. They continue dancing around the circle until they dance with all members of the opposite sex. The foot pattern is danced to the clave as they rotate partners, while moving around the circle. The men move clockwise and the women move counter-clockwise.[43]

THREE SALSA CENTERS

New York City became the birthplace of salsa and remains a mecca because of its immense number of Puerto Rican immigrants. A more

TIPS FOR DANCING SALSA

It is extremely important to make a connection with your partner when dancing salsa. Without this body language rapport, you cannot lead, and she cannot follow. Your frame is also very important. Stand facing your partner with your palms touching hers. Gently push her away from you. She should push back with even pressure, not allowing her arms to move. This exercise will give you a sense of what leading and following feels like. You can also dance the basic steps in a ballroom practice position with your arms extended, palms resting on her shoulders, and with her arms extended, palms resting on your shoulders. This practice position will keep your frame stable as you develop muscle memory of the basic steps.

You must lead your partner through the turns and patterns and not try to force her to execute them. It is important to show her where and when to move. Your partner will not enjoy trying to catch up without a clue about what is coming next. Learn to be a good leader. Then work on your styling.

Salsa music tells a story, and you can synchronize your movements to the musical phrases of this story. It is important to match steps to the music at the appropriate times. Some patterns and turns fit with the slow sections of the music, whereas others are more suitable to dance during the fast segments of the music. It is also important to know when the music is going to end. You want to finish the dance with an impressive dip or to emphasize the final beat of the music with your most outstanding step.

recent influx of Dominican immigrants has kept the trend alive. Miami is a salsa stronghold because of the large population of Cuban immigrants. The country of Colombia is a transnational hub for the salsa. Cali, Colombia, is known for its hot salsa dancing. Today, Cali's seniors are dancing the salsa at dance clubs called **viejotecas**, which means dance clubs for old people. The viejotecas open early, charge a low price for admission, and play classic salsa music. There are more than 90 of these clubs officially registered. Cali salsa has its own essence; it is fast, and dancers pick up their feet, executing excellent turns. The most authentic Cali salsa is danced at the viejotecas. The seniors' love of authentic Cali salsa is spreading to young people, who are now coming to the clubs to learn the old dance and to dance an important part of their local culture while preserving it. Upscale clubs are now hosting viejoteca nights. They charge a fraction of the usual entrance fee, put away the pop-influenced salsa of today, and play the classics.

INTERNATIONAL SALSA CONGRESSES

The term *salsa congress*, which is used to describe a salsa festival that meets some of the requirements of a professional conference, was first coined in 1997 at the initial congress in Puerto Rico. Today, congresses are held in most countries around the world. A congress features salsa exhibitions, workshops, social dance parties, live bands, booths with exhibitors selling products and accessories, master classes, and, frequently, competitions.

Salsa is evolving as both a social and ballroom dance. From Latin dance venues to televised dance competitions it continues to grow in popularity worldwide. As an international favorite, where there is dancing, there is salsa.

CHRONOLOGY

Pre-1492	Amerindian areito ceremonies are performed.
1492	Christopher Columbus claims Quisqueya for Spain.
1492–1697	Spain rules Quisqueya.
1494	Portugal gets Brazil through the Treaty of Tordesillas.
1502	Rio de Janeiro is discovered.
1511	Diego Velazquez de Cuéllar settles Cuba.
1536	Buenos Aires is founded by the Spanish.
1580	Buenos Aires is founded again by the Spanish.
1600s	The Taino Indians disappear.
1697	Spain cedes the western part of Quisqueya to France.
1763–1960	Rio de Janeiro becomes the capital of Brazil. Late 1700s: Araucanian Indians still roam the Pampa.
1790s	Haitians introduce contredanse into Cuba.
1791–1803	Haitian revolution ends French rule.
1795	The French conquer the Dominican Republic.
1803	The Louisiana Purchase takes place.
1816	The waltz arrives in Buenos Aires.

1822–1844	The Dominican Republic is occupied by an independent Haiti.
1840	The first Carnival parade is performed in Brazil.
1844	Independence for the Dominican Republic.
	Merengue típico emerges.
1878	Araucanian Indians move out of the Pampa in Argentina.
1879	Miguel Faílde composes the first danzón score.
	Danzón is the Cuban national dance until the 1930s.
	The Cuban rumba evolves.
1882	Maxixe is documented in Brazil.
1888	The abolition of slavery occurs in Brazil.
1890	Capoeira is outlawed in Brazil.
1890s	Maxixe becomes Rio de Janeiro's primary Carnival dance.
Early 1900s	The samba evolves in Brazil.
1909	The tango becomes a popular dance in Argentina.
1913	The tango arrives in Helsinki and becomes national dance of Finland.
	The tango a la francesa returns to Argentina.
1913–1914	The tango invades Paris.
1915–1934	The United States occupies Haiti.
1916–1924	The U.S. Marine Corps occupies the Dominican Republic.
1917	Son appears in Havana.
1919	Maxixe is the most popular dance in urban Brazil.

1920s	Maxixe is forbidden in Brazil.
	Argentina becomes one of the wealthiest nations in the world.
1921	Rudolph Valentino dances the tango in two Hollywood films.
1928	The first samba school opens in Brazil.
1930	Rafael Trujillo begins a 31-year dictatorship in Dominican Republic.
1930s	Katherine Dunham conducts Caribbean dance research in Haiti.
	The tango is out of date in Paris, but it's in its golden age in Argentina.
	Capoeira is recognized as a martial art and a national sport in Brazil.
1932	The first Capoeira school opens in Brazil.
1936	Rafael Trujillo declares Cibao merengue the national music and dance of the Dominican Republic.
	Researchers begin codifying folkloric dance in Cuba, the Dominican Republic, and Haiti.
	The tango is at the height of its popularity in Argentina.
	Samba de gafieira appears in Brazil.
1941	The Bureau of Ethnology is created in Haiti.
1943	Pérez Prado introduces mambo music to Havana.
1947	A political coup is performed by Dumarsais Estimé in Haiti.
1947–early 1950	The mambo craze hits the United States.
1950s	The golden age of tango ends.

Rumba catches on and son, mambo, and cha-cha-chá are popular in the United States.

Enrique Jorrin introduces cha-cha-chá to Cuba.

1953–1989   Katherine Dunham works with folkloric dancers in Haiti.

1955   Konpa direk (compas) appears in Haiti.

1959   The Cuban Revolution occurs.

1960s   Bachata is developed in the Dominican countryside.

The tango declines in Argentina as the youth begin to prefer rock music.

The bossa nova emerges in Brazil.

Salsa emerges in the United States.

1961   Rafael Trujillo is assassinated.

1964   Fania Records emerges in the United States.

1976   *Billboard* features "Salsa Explosion" in the United States.

1977   DanceBrazil established in the United States.

1980s   The recording industry prospers in the Dominican Republic.

Lambada evolves from the samba in Brazil.

Merengue becomes popular in the United States.

1983   *Tango Argentino* opens in Paris.

1984   The Sambadrome is built in Rio de Janeiro.

1985   The tango is revitalized.

Tango Argentino opens on and off-Broadway.

The tango is revitalized in Argentina.

1990s   Bachata loses its lower-class image and becomes popular in the Dominican Republic.

1997 The Buena Vista Social Club album and film are produced.

1998 Johnny Ventura is elected mayor of Santo Domingo in the Dominican Republic.

2005 UNESCO names the Bahian samba da roda a "Heritage of Humanity."

NOTES

CHAPTER 1

1 Susanna Sloat, ed, *Caribbean Dance from Abakua to Zouk: How Movement Shapes Identity* (Gainesville: University of Florida Press, 2002), ix.

2 John Charles Chasteen, *National Rhythms, African Roots: The Deep History of Latin American Popular Dance* (Albuquerque: University of New Mexico Press, 2004), 156.

3 Peter Manuel, *Caribbean Currents: Caribbean Music from Rumba to Reggae* (Philadelphia, PA: Temple University Press, 2009), 3.

4 Sloat, x.

5 Chasteen, 3.

6 The Life and Work of Katherine Dunham. Available online at http://www.loc.gov/loc/lcib/0412/dunham.html.

CHAPTER 2

7 Sloat, 31.

8 Ibid., 33.

9 Manuel, 21.

10 Ibid., 29.

11 Sloat, 49.

12 Ibid., 50.

13 Ibid., 44.

14 Manuel, 54.

15 Ibid.

16 Ibid., 48.

17 Ibid., 60.

18 Sloat, 27.

CHAPTER 3

19 Sloat, 127.

20 Manuel, 121.

21 Ibid., 118–119.

22 Ibid., 121.

23 Ibid., 122.

24 Ibid., 124.

25 Ibid., 132.

26 Ibid., 135.

CHAPTER 4

27 Sloat, xiv.
28 Haitian Dance, Folklore, and Tradition. Available online at http://www.haitiantreasures.com/HT_agoci.dance.htm
29 Sloat, 110–111.

CHAPTER 5

30 Simon Collier, Artemis Cooper, Maria Susana Azzi, and Richard Martin, *Tango: The Dance, the Song, the Story* (London: Thames and Hudson), 41.
31 Ibid., 169.
32 Chasteen, 6.
33 Collier, 380.

CHAPTER 6

34 Chasteen, 26.
35 Maya Talmon-Chvaicer, *The Hidden History of Capoeira: A Collision of Cultures in the Brazilian Battle Dance* (Austin: University of Texas Press, 2008), 1 and 115.
36 Barbara Browning. *Samba: Resistance in Motion: Arts and Politics of the Everyday* (Bloomington: Indiana University Press, 1995), 1.
37 Ibid., xxiv and xxv.

CHAPTER 8

38 Manuel, 45.
39 Ibid., 99.
40 Ibid., 125.
41 Ibid., 91.
42 Ibid., 106.
43 Chasteen, 10.

GLOSSARY

abakuá   An urban Afro-Cuban ethnic and religious brotherhood from the West African Calabar region

affranchi   A class of Haitian freemen

Amerindians   American Indians

arará   A Cuban dance and music tradition from West Africa

Araucanian Indians   A member of a group of Indian peoples of south central Chile and adjacent regions of Argentina

Arawak   Another name for Taino Indians

areíto   Arawak social and religious ceremonies that served to preserve oral history and broadcast news through music and dance

attambor   A drum made from a hollowed-out tree trunk with holes in it for resonance and deep grooves along the entire length but without any stretched hide or skin

bachata   A romantic bolero style couple's dance from the Dominican Republic

balada   Sentimental Spanish song sung in pop style

banda   A vodou dance of the Guédé spirits of the life-and-death cycle

bandoneon   The characteristic tango instrument, cousin of the accordion, brought to Argentina from Germany in the late nineteenth century

batá   A two-headed drum (one head is larger than the other) played in trios in Afro-Cuban santería music

batárumba   A recent Cuban development combining rumba with yoruba batá drumming

bateria Formation of musicians at the head or mouth of the roda in capoeira

bembé Dance party associated with the Afro-Cuban Santería religion

berimbaus Stringed bows used in traditional capoeira music

bolero A slow Spanish Caribbean couple's dance in 4/4 time

bossa nova Short-lived dance craze of the 1960s with some elements of samba

cabildos African ethnic and religious associations in Cuba

call and response A chorus responding to the lead of a solo singer

candombé An Afro-Argentine dance with powerful and energetic movements performed by men

candomble An African religion featuring dance in honor of the gods

cantos Improvised rumba lyrics

capoeira Afro-Brazilian art form that combines martial arts, music, dance, and games

capoeiras (capoeirista, singular) People who play capoeira

carabalí A music and dance tradition in Cuba from the Calabar region in Africa

carimbó A sensual Brazilian dance

Carnival (Karnival) The three-day to week-long period preceding Lent on the Catholic calendar. It is celebrated with parades featuring floats and elaborately costumed dancers and musicians.

casino Contemporary salsa in Cuba. It is danced by couples.

casino de la rueda (salsa whelo) A Cuban casino salsa in which generally four couples in a circle dance patterns in unison with their own partners and other couples, circling until they have danced with each person of the opposite sex

cha-cha-chá A popular Cuban social dance featuring three quick steps followed by two slow steps

chamada Interruption in capoeira, as the more proficient player or teacher points out opportunities to strike to the less proficient player. It is one of the ways masters and professors teach new players.

chula A call-and-response song in capoeira

Cibao Valley   Densely populated area of the North Central Dominican Republic

Ciboney Indians   Indigenous peoples of the Caribbean

cinquillo   A rhythmic pattern containing five pulses within three beats. It is related to the development of the Cuban clave.

clave   Two cylindrical pieces of hardwood that are hit against each other. This simple percussion instrument is the pillar of Latin music, providing the principal pulsating beat of rhythmic timing.

cocktail samba   A variation of the samba de gafieira

Columbia   A type of Cuban rumba danced by men

compadres   Men engaged in herding cattle from the pampa to the slaughter house. They maintained gaucho attitudes.

compadritos   An unflattering term for poor young native Argentinean men who imitated the behavior and attitudes of the compadres. They were identifiable by the slouched hat, neckerchief (called a *lengue*), knife, and high-heeled boots that they wore.

compas (konpa direk)   Haitian creolized form of the mereng

Congo (Kongo-Angolian)   An African music and dance tradition in Cuba

conquistadores   The leaders of the Spanish conquest of the Americas in the sixteenth century. They exploited the Native Americans.

contradanza Francesa   The most frequently performed colonial dance in Cuba

contredanse   French court dances that are also called contra dances; they evolved from the English country dance and were taken to Cuba by French and Haitian colonists.

corners   The couple to either side of a couple in the four-couple Cuban casino salsa

corridas   Walking steps done by male candombe dancers

corridos   A series of songs sung during a capoeira game

corte y quebrada   A name for the milonga dance technique

cotillions   A ballroom dance for couples. It resembles the quadrille.

Creole language   A mixture of African and European languages

Cuban hip motion   The rhythmic swaying of the hips caused by the bending and straightening of the knees as steps are taken

cumbia   Colombian traditional dance and music

dambalah   A spirit that is the source of energy and life. It is represented by a serpent.

danymé   Dance similar to capoeira. It is practiced in Martinique.

danzón   Cuban nineteenth-century national dance that had alternating walking and dancing patterns

décima   Spanish song structure based on a 10-syllable line within a 10-line stanza

desperlote   Female-dominated form of casino de la rueda in Cuba

diablos cojuelos   Devils in the Dominican Republic Carnival

Djuba/Martinique   A vodou dance from the Djuba nation

folkloric (Folklórico)   Traditional dance of the country

foxtrot   A ballroom dance that includes slow walking steps and quick running steps

gafieira   Popular urban nightclubs of Rio de Janeiro in the 1940s

gauchos   Nomadic horsemen of the Argentinean pampa. Their lifestyle was on the edge of and frequently beyond the limits of society.

ginga   A swaying dance movement in the capoeira

guaguancó   The most popular style of the rumba

güiros   An instrument inherited from the indigenous Taino culture and made from a dried gourd; it is scraped to make its sound.

habanera   A popular Cuban creole rhythm and dance derived from the contradanza and combined with African rhythms

Ibo   A vodou dance representing the Ibo nation of Nigeria

jaleo   A lively, extended call-and-response section in the merengue típico cibaeño

kongo   A vodou dance associated with the Congo nation

kouzin   A spirit honored in Djuba/Martinique dance

Kreyòl ayisyen   The Haitian Creole language

ladainha   The opening litanylike song in the capoeira

ladjo   A dance similar to the capoeira practiced in Martinique

lambada   A sensual Brazilian couple's dance of the 1980s; it evolved from the samba.

Latin America   Countries in the Americas whose language is derived from Latin: Spanish, Portuguese, and French

louvação   Call-and-response songs in the capoeira

lundu   A West African dance from which samba was derived

lunfardo   An expressive Italian-based local vocabulary that had the strongest influence on the modern colloquial Spanish of Buenos Aires. It tells a story in the song lyrics of the tango.

lwa   African spirits honored in vodou music and dance

malandragem   The art of trickery in the capoeira

malicia   Trickery or deceit in the capoeira

mambo   A popular Cuban social dance derived from the son

mambonicks   Mambo-happy dancers in New York City

mani   A mock dance battle in Cuba similar to the capoeira

maracas   Gourds filled with small stones

maxixe   An Afro-Brazilian dance in 2/4 time. It is known as the Brazilian tango.

mayohuacan   Drum made from a hollowed-out log with H-shaped tongues cut into it

mazurka   A lively Polish dance for couples

mereng   A Haitian-Creole dance based on a five-note rhythm

merengue   The most important music and dance genre of the Dominican Republic, consisting of a two-step pattern

mestizos   People of mixed European and indigenous Amerindian blood

milat   Light-skinned Haitian Affranchi freemen

milonga   An Argentinean close-embrace-style social dance popular in the 1870s. It can also refer to a place or an event where tango is danced.

minuets   European court dances from the sixteenth and seventeenth centuries. They were performed by colonists in the Americas.

montuno Call-and-response portion of Cuban music found in the rumba and the salsa

nago A vodou dance from Nagos of the interior of the former Slave Coast of Africa

ngoma A single-headed drum used to play Congo music associated with the Cuban Palo religion

nwa Dark-skinned Haitian Affranchi freemen

orishas Divinities that enter the bodies of worshipers and dance fiercely

palmadas Flamenco-style rhythmic hand claps

palo An Afro-Dominican drum made from a hollowed-out tree trunk; also called atabal. When capitalized, it refers to an Afro-Caribbean religion.

Pampa An extensive, generally grass-covered plain of temperate South America east of the Andes

parigol A variation of the Yanvalou associated with La Sirene, the Mermaid

pasadias Sunday afternoon fiestas in the Dominican Republic

paseo A Spanish dance structure of walking elegantly to the music

payadores Folk-singers of the Pampa who played an important role in the disappearing world of the gaucho

petro A vodou dance associated with the Haitian revolution

pidgin Simplified speech used for communication between people of different languages. It is a language created by the blending of two or more previous languages. These languages are usually created by people who meet in a place that is the original homeland of neither.

polka A simple waltzlike dance originating in the Czech Republic

polyrhythms (polymeter or cross rhythms) The simultaneous combination of contrasting rhythms in a musical composition when two or more regular beat patterns are combined

quadrille A set dance brought to the Caribbean by the French

rara Haitian festival held during Lent

roda The circle where capoeira is played

rumba   The most famous and significant Afro-Cuban secular music and dance form

rumberos   Authentic rumba performers

salsa   Music and dance originating in New York in the 1960s

salsa dura   The original hard-driving salsa

salsa romantica   A sweet, sentimental salsa sound popular in the 1980s

salsa whelo   Cuban salsa in the round

salsero   A male salsa dancer

samba   A Brazilian dance with Kongo-Angolan heritage

samba axé   Solo samba danced to axé rhythm

samba de gafieira   Brazilian ballroom samba

samba de roda   A traditional Afro-Brazilian dance that accompanies the ceremonial aspects of a capoeira game

samba duro   A battle dance from El Salvador

samba no pé   A solo Brazilian carnival dance

samba pagode   A dance resembling the samba de gafieira but more subdued and intimate

samba reggae   The samba with the reggae drumbeat added to traditional samba music

samba rock   A Latin nightclub dance that resembles a mix of the samba de gafieira and the salsa

santería   A Cuban religion derived from Yoruba beliefs

schottische   A dance derived from one of Poland's five national dances, the krakowiak from the region of Kraków. It is characterized by a smooth running step punctuated by slight hops, heel clicks and foot stamps, and very fast turns.

semba   A traditional Angolan dance

shimmying   A dance technique that employs a shaking of the body from the shoulders down

shines   Steps performed on the beat of the clave while dancing apart from a partner

son A popular twentieth-century Cuban music and dance style

syncopation Rhythmic interest and complexity created by regular beats (silent or heard) and offbeat accents

Taino Indians Indigenous Indians of the Caribbean; also called Arawak

tango A ballroom dance of Latin American origin in 4/4 time. It is characterized by long pauses and stylized body positions.

tango liso A smooth tango

tangomania An obsession with tango

tangueros Male tango dancers

tres A Cuban offshoot of the guitar

tumba Francesa (French drum) Haitian-influenced stylistic tradition of African-derived music and dance in Cuba

twoubadou A Haitian secular-style dance that affected the development of konpa direk

vacunano A part of the rumba in which a pelvic thrust, graceful kick, or swat is directed toward the woman's groin

Vaslav Nijinsky A famous early twentieth-century ballet dancer and choreographer

viejotecas Colombian salsa clubs for senior citizens

vodou (voodoo, vodun, vodoun) Afro-Haitian religion primarily of Dahomian and Congolese derivation

waltz A European couple's dance in three-quarter meter

West Indies A large group of islands that separate the Caribbean Sea from the Atlantic Ocean

yambú A type of Cuban rumba

yanvalou A vodou dance from Benin; it honors all the spirits of the Rada nation.

yoruba A Cuban rhythm from southwestern Nigeria

zaka A vodou dance that depicts the hard labor of work in the fields

zapateo   A specific Cuban folk dance of Spanish derivation featuring heel stamping to syncopated music or any percussive movement of the feet. It is derived from Spanish dance.

zarenyen   A vodou dance of the Guédé spirit family of death

zemba queca   A graceful Brazilian dance form danced in closed position that mixed with the maxixe and evolved into the samba

BIBLIOGRAPHY

Browning, Barbara. *Samba: Resistance in Motion: Arts and Politics of the Everyday*. Bloomington: Indiana University Press, 1995.

Chasteen, John Charles. *National Rhythms, African Roots: The Deep History of Latin American Popular Dance*. Albuquerque: University of New Mexico Press, 2004.

———. *Born in Blood and Fire: A Concise History of Latin America*. New York: Norton, 2001.

Collier, Simon, Artemis Cooper, Maria Susana Azzi, and Richard Martin. *Tango: The Dance, the Song, the Story*. London: Thames and Hudson, 1995.

Innocent, Rol'hans. *Haitian Dance, Folklore, and Tradition*, accessed at http://www.haitiantreasures.com/HT_agoci.dance.htm, February 10, 2010.

Manuel, Peter. *Caribbean Currents: Caribbean Music from Rumba to Reggae*. Philadelphia: Temple University Press, 2006.

Sloat, Susanna, ed. *Caribbean Dance from Abakua to Zouk: How Movement Shapes Identity*. Gainesville: University of Florida Press, 2002.

Selected Chronology, accessed at http://www.katherinedunham.org/, February 10, 2010.

Talmon-Chvaicer, Maya. *The Hidden History of Capoeira: A Collision of Cultures in the Brazilian Battle Dance*. Austin: University of Texas Press, 2008.

The Life and Work of Katherine Dunham, Dancer-Choreographer Subject of New Web Presentation, accessed at http://www.loc.gov/loc/lcib/0412/dunham.html, October 5, 2009.

FURTHER RESOURCES

BOOKS

Alegria, Ricardo and Jose Arrom. *Taino: Pre-Columbian Art and Culture from the Caribbean*. New York: Monacelli Press, 1998.

Aschenbrenner, Joyce. *Katherine Dunham: Dancing a Life*. Urbana: University of Illinois Press, 2002.

Capoeira, Nestor. *Capoeira: Roots of the Dance-Fight-Game*. Berkeley, CA: North Atlantic Books, 2002.

Denniston, Christine. *The Meaning of Tango: The Story of the Argentinian Dance*. London: Portico, 2007.

Manuel, Peter, ed. *Creolizing Contradance in the Caribbean*. Philadelphia: Temple University Press, 2009.

Roberts, John Storm. *The Latin Tinge: The Impact of Latin American Music on the United States*. New York: Oxford University Press, 1999.

WEB SITES

Argentine Tango
> *http://www.elportaldeltango.com/english/frnews.htm*
> This site is available in English and Spanish and contains dance history, a film list, and traditional tango music played by famous orchestras.

Buena Vista Social Club: Official Site of the Legendary Musicians
> *http://www.buenavistasocialclub.com/.*
> This site includes photos and an MP3 sampling of berimbau music, the lyrics, and translations of some songs.

Capoeira
> *http://www.capoeirista.com/*
> This site contains capoeira information, music, and a listing of teachers.

Cuba

http://www.cubanfolkloricdance.com/home.php

This site has video clips of many Cuban folkloric dances in the Cutumba section. In the CD/DVD section, the viewer can preview and purchase music and instructional DVDs.

Carnival of the Dominican Republic

http://www.videojug.com/film/the-carnavale-of-dominican-republic

This site shows footage from the Carnival and briefly describes costumes.

Dominican Republic

http://domrep.org/documents/DominicanRepublicHistory.pdf

This site tells a brief history of the Dominican Republic and of the merengue.

Haitian Treasures

http://www.haitiantreasures.com/HT_agoci.dance.htm

Typical vodou dances are described by Rol'hans Innocent, Artistic Director of Agoci Entertainment. *The Haitian Vodou Ritual Dances and Their Secularization* (VHS) is available for preview and purchase.

Johnny Ventura—Merenguero

http://www.youtube.com/watch?v=7XzINu2ee4A

This site shows Johnny Ventura performing the *merenguero hasta la tambora.*

Katherine Dunham

http://lcweb2.loc.gov/diglib/ihas/html/dunham/dunham-home.html

This is the Library of Congress's site about the Life and Work of Katherine Dunham: Dancer-Choreographer.

Salsa

http://www.salsacongress.com/

This site lists salsa congresses and festivals around the world.

Salsa New York

http://www.salsanewyork.com

This site contains a salsa "on two" dancer's guide and magazine.

Samba

http://www.youtube.com/watch?v=K3mYDwRTALo

This is a 10-minute sample of the Carnival samba parade in Rio de Janeiro.

VIDEOGRAPHY

Capoeira

Only the Strong, 20th Century Fox, 1993.

Cuba

Mambo Kings, Warner Brothers, 1992.

Dominican Republic

SOY: Johnny Ventura, Ares Multimedia, 2005.

Haiti

The Haitian Vodou Ritual Dances and Their Secularization, Haitian Treasures, 2004.

Salsa

Salsa: The Motion Picture, Cannon Films, 1988.

Dance with Me, Columbia Pictures, 1998.

Samba

Brazil: Priestesses, Samba Dancers, and Mulattos of Brazil, Princeton, NJ: Films for the Humanities and Sciences, 2003.

Samba on Your Feet: The Documentary, Patagonia Film Group, 2006.

Tango

Cafe de Los Maestros, Lita Stantic Producciones, 2008.

Tango, Sony Pictures, 1998.

PICTURE CREDITS

PAGE

16: © Infobase Publishing
18: © Scala/White Images/ Art Resource, NY
21: © AFP/Getty Images
27: © Infobase Publishing
30: © James Quine/Alamy
34: © Barry Lewis/Alamy
39: © Time & Life Pictures/ Getty Images
43: © Infobase Publishing
45: © Jon McLean/Alamy
48: © Getty Images
52: © Stock Connection Blue/ Alamy
56: © AFP/Getty Images
60: © Chad Ehlers/Alamy
64: © Infobase Publishing
65: © AFP/Getty Images
72: © Infobase Publishing
74: © LatinContent/Getty Images
76: © Globo via Getty Images
79: © Peter M. Wilson/Alamy
83: © Julie Lemberger/Corbis
87: © ABC via Getty Images
90: © LOOK Die Bildagentur der Fotografen GmbH/ Alamy

INDEX

A

Abakuá dance, 29, 35
accordions, 66
affranchi class, 50
affranchi mereng, 51
African slaves
    Brazil and, 70–71, 75, 78–79
    Cuba and, 28–30
    Dominican Republic and, 41–42
    influences of, 19, 20, 22–25
Agoci Entertainment, 52
Aguilar, Pedro "Cuban Pete", 38
Agwe, 54
Ailey, Alvin, 82
Alvin Ailey American Dance Theater, 54
Amerindians, 17
Anthony, Marc, 46
Antonio de Marchi (Baron), 67
Arará rhythms, 29
Araucanian Indians, 58, 62
Arawak Indians. *See* Taino Indians
areíto dances, 17
Argentina
    Carnival in, 20
    compadritos, candombe and, 61–62
    overview of, 58
    tango and, 66–67
    wealth and immigration in, 62–63
Ash Wednesday, 20, 51
Assante, Armand, 38
attambor, 17

B

Bacchus, 20
bachata, 47–49
Bahian samba de roda, 75
balada, 46
Balaguer, Joaqúin, 46
Ballet de Camagüey, 40
Ballet Nacional de Cuba, 40
ballroom dancing, 66–67, 75, 77
Banda, 54, 55
Banderas, Antonio, 38
bandoneon, 66
baptisms, 84
Barretto, Ray, 86
Barrio Norte, 63, 67
batá drums, 29, 35
Batárumba, 35
bateria, 81
battle dances, 84
bembé, 29
berimbaus, 81
Billboard, 87
Bimba, 80
Blanchet, Lina, 53

Blood and Sand, 68
bolero, 32–33
bossa nova, 77
Brazil
    capoeira and, 78–84
    Carnival in, 20–21
    maxixe and, 71
    overview of, 70–71
    samba and, 73–77
Brazilian tango. *See* Maxixe
brazilwood, 71, 78
Broadway, 65
Brown, James, 48
Browning, Barbara, 73
The Buena Vista Social Club, 40
Bureau of Ethnology, 53
Bwa Cayiman, 55

C

"El Caballo", 48–49
cabildos, 28
Cal Tjader Quintet, 86
Cali salsa, 91
call-and-response-style chants, 17, 23, 33, 42, 81
Campo, Pupi, 36
candombe, 61–62
candomblé, 73
cantos, 33
capoeira, 78–84
capoeira Angola, 80
capoeira regional style, 80
capoeira schools, 73

capoeiras, defined, 78
Carabalí rhythms, 29
Caribbean island folkloric dance, 24
carimbó, 75
Carmen, 31
Carnival
    Argentina and, 67
    Brazil and, 70, 72, 73
    Haiti and, 51
    overview of, 20–22
casino de la rueda, 37, 90
casino salsa, 89–90
casino-style salsa, 37
Catskill Mountains, 38
cha-cha-chá, 24, 32, 36–37
chamada, 84
chants, call-and-response, 17, 23, 33, 42, 81
chula, 81
Cibao Valley, 42–43
Ciboney Indians, 26–27, 41
Cidade Nova, 71
cinquillo rhythm, 31, 32
claves, 31–33, 35, 89–90
clubs, 88, 91
cocktail samba, 75
Colombia, 91
Columbia dance, 35
Columbus, Christopher, 26, 41
communism, 37
compadres, 61
compadritos, 60, 61–62
companies, 40, 56–57
compas (konpa direk), 51
competitive dances, 35, 37, 67
Congo, 54
Congo music and dance, 22–23
Congo rhythms, 28
congresses, 91
Conjunto Folklórico Cutumba, 40

Conjunto Folklórico de Oriente, 40
Conjunto Folklórico Nacional de Cuba, 40
conquistadores, 27
contra dance, See *contradanza Francesa* and *contredanse.*
contradanza Francesa, 19, 28, 30, 31
contredanse, 19, 28, 51
Cooder, Ry, 40
corners, 90
corridas, 61
corridos, 81
cortes y quebrada, 62, 63
costumes, Carnival and, 22
Creole French language, 28, 50–51
creolized dances, 19–22, 42
criminal activity, 79–80
Cuba
    African influences on, 28–30
    bolero and, 32–33
    capoeira and, 84
    Carnival in, 22
    cha-cha-chá and, 36–37
    claves and, 31–32
    contradanza in, 19
    Cuban Revolution and, 37, 40
    danzón and, 31
    European influences on, 27–28
    habanera and, 30–31
    indigenous dances of, 26–27
    mambo and, 36
    overview of, 26
    rumba and, 33–36
    salsa and, 86, 89–90
    son and, 32
    training of dancers in, 40

Cuban hip motion, 48
Cugat, Xavier, 36
cumbia, 85

D

Dambalah, 54
dance companies, 40, 56–57
DanceBrazil, 82
The Dances of Haiti (Dunham), 25
DanceSport competitions, 67
danymé, 84
Danza Contemporánea de Cuba, 40
danzón, 31, 42, 61, 62
décima lyrics, 27, 33
desperlote, 37
diabolito, 29
d'Incamps, Olivier Lamotte, 77
Dionysus, 20
Djuba/Martinique, 54, 55
Dominican Republic
    bachata and, 47–49
    Carnival in, 22
    merengue tipico and, 42–45
    modern merengue and, 46–47
    overview of, 41–42
Donay, Millie, 38
dos Reis Machado, Manuel, 80
Dowell, Anthony, 68
Dunham, Katherine, 24–25, 53, 54

E

"Échale Salsita" (Piñeiro), 85
El Salvador, 84
Elegba, 30
embargos, 37
emotion, dance and, 10–13
Española, 41, 50

Estimé, Dumarsais, 53
European influences,
    17–22, 27–28, 51
The Event of the Year, 11–13
exercise, 77
extravaganza dance, 40

F

Faílde, Miguel, 31
Fania Records, 86–88
Feet of Rhythm, 56–57
Finland, 66
fire dances, 55
Flamenco hand claps, 32
flogging, 79
folkloric dance, 24
*The Four Horsemen of the
    Apocalypse*, 68
foxtrot, 42
France, 42, 50
Frank, Henry, 54
French contradance, 19,
    28, 30
French court dances, 28
French Drum, 28
Freyre, Gilberto, 80

G

gafieira, 75
games, 81
gauchos, 58
George, Sergio, 87
ginga, 83
Greece, 20
guaguancó, 35
Gualeguaychú, Argentina,
    20
Guéde, 55
Guevara, Che, 37
güiros, 32
guitars, 32

H

habanera, 20, 30–31, 59–60
Haiti
    Carnival in, 20–21, 51
    contredanse in, 19

Dominican Republic
    and, 42
Dunham and, 24–25
French colonials and, 28
mambo and, 36
overview of, 50–53
vodoun religion and,
    52–57
Haiti Chante et Danse, 53
Haitian Creole language,
    50–51
Harlow, Larry, 86
harmony, 24
hip movements, 48, 62, 77
Hispaniola. *See* Dominican
    Republic; Haiti
Home of the Mambo, 38
hymns, 24

I

Ibo, 54
Iglesias, Julio, 46
immigrants, 62–63, 87–88,
    91–92
Imperial Society of
    Teachers of Dancing, 77
improvisation, 33, 60
Indian culture, 17
indigenous dances, 17, 23,
    26–27
initiation rites, 53
Innocent, Rol'hans, 52
International Dance
    Teachers Association, 77
Island Possessed
    (Dunham), 25
Italianization, 63–66
Iwa, 51

J

jaleo, 42
Japan, 77
Jean-Baptiste, Nemours, 51
jogo, 81, 84
Jorrín, Enrique, 36
Journey to Accompong
    (Dunham), 25

Julius Rosenwald Fund,
    24

K

kettledrums, 31
Kongo, 54
konpa direk, 51
Kouzin, 55

L

ladainhas, 81
ladjá, 84
lambada, 75–77
languages
    Cuba and, 28
    Haiti and, 50–51
    Latin America and, 15
    rumba and, 33
    tango and, 58, 63
Latin America, overview
    of, 15–17
Legba Singers, 53
lengue, 61
Lent, 20, 51
line dances, 19
Lora, Nico, 42
louvação, 81
Loza, Steven, 38
lundu, 72
lunfardo, 63
lyrics
    bachata and, 47
    merengue and, 42
    rumba and, 33
    salsa and, 88
    tango and, 63

M

Machito, 36, 38
Magloire, Paul Eugene, 53
Makandal Company,
    56–57
malandragem, 81
malicia, 81
mambo, 32, 36, 38–39, 42
Mambo (voodoo
    priestess), 36

Mambo Kings, 38
"Mambo on the One", 89
mambonicks, 38
maracas, 17, 32
Marchi, Antonio de, 67
martial arts, 79, 80
Martinique, 84
mask dances, 29
masks, Carnival and, 20
Masucci, Jerry, 86
Mater Dolorosa, 53
maxixe, 24, 61, 62, 71, 77
mayohuacan, 17
mazurka, 19
mereng, 51
merengue, 24, 42–49
merengue tipico, 42–45
merengue típico cibaeño, 42, 44
mestizos, 82
Mestra Bimba, 80
Michael (student), 11–13
milat, 50
militias, 80
milonga, 60–62
minuets, 28
modern merengue, 46–47
Molas, Ricardo Rodriguez, 58
montuno, 33
movies, 68–69
"La muerte del chivo", 44
multinational corporations, 46
Murphy, Eddie, 82

N

Nago, 54, 55
Napoleon Bonaparte III, 15
national dance companies, 40, 56–57
National Dance Institute, 11–13
National Heritage Fellowships, 82
ngoma drums, 28

Nigeia, 54–55
Nijinsky, Vaslav, 68
Nureyev, Rudolf, 68
nwa, 50

O

on two dancers, 89
Orfeo Negro, 82
organs, 66
orishas, 29

P

Pacheco, Johnny, 86
Palladium Ballroom, 38
palmadas, 32
Palmares, 78–79
Palo religion, 28
Pampa, 58, 60, 62
Paraguay, 80
partnering turns, 39
pasadias, 42
paseo, 31, 42
paso de la empalizada, 47
payadores, 60
Pelé, 82
perigol, 54
Petro, 54, 55
pidgin, 58
Piñeiro, Ignacio, 85
polka, 19, 51
polyrhythms, 22, 33, 88
Portugal, 70–71
Portuguese language, 15, 58
Prado, Pérez, 36
pretzels, 90
"La protesta", 42
Puente, Tito, 36, 38
Puerto Rico, 86, 87–88, 90

Q

quadrilles, 19, 28, 51
quebrada, 62
quintos, 35
Quisqueya, 41, 50

R

radio, 86
rara bands, 21

reggae, 75, 77
Regla de Ocha, 29–30
Reis, Juca, 80
religious ceremonies, 17
rhythms. *See also*
   Polyrhythms; *Specific rhythms*
      of Afro-Cuban music and dance, 28–29
      bachata and, 47
      samba and, 73, 75
      vodou dance and, 53
Rio de Janeiro, Brazil, 20–21, 71–73, 80
Rio de la Plata, 63–64
"Ripped Parrot", 42
rituals, 23, 51. *See also*
   Vodoun religion
Riverside Dance Festival, 82
Roca, Julio Argentino, 62
rodas, 81
Rodrígues, Tito, 36, 38
Rodriguez, Arsenio, 85
Roman Catholicism, 52–53
Rome, 20
Rosenwald Fund, 24
Roumain, Jacques, 53
round dances, 19
rumba, 33–36
rumberos, 35
"the runs", 12–13

S

Sabado de la rumba, 35
salsa
   contemporary Cuban, 89–90
   Cuba and, 37
   Dominican Republic and, 47
   Fania Records and, 86–88
   international congresses and, 92
   mambo and, 39

roots of, 85–86
shines and, 89
spreading popularity of, 24
three centers of, 91–92
tips for dancing, 91
as variation of son, 32
Salsa (Harlow), 86
salsa congress, 91
salsa dura, 47
"Salsa Explosion", 86–87
salsa in the round, 37, 90
salsa romantica, 47
salsa whelo, 37, 90
Salvador da Bahia, Brazil, 20
samba, 20, 24, 72–77
samba axé, 75
samba da gafieira, 75
samba da roda, 75, 82
samba duro, 84
samba no pé, 73–75
samba pagode, 75
Samba Parade, 20
samba reggae, 75, 77
samba rock, 75
Samba Runway, 73
Sambadrome Stadium, 20, 73
Sampaio Ferraz, Joao Batista, 80
Santería, 29–30
Santería dances, 28
Santo Domingo, 41–42, 46
Satanism, 56
schottische, 19
semba dance, 20
set dances, 19
shantytowns, 46
shimmying, 36
shines, 89
Silk Road, 70
La Sirené, 54
Slave Coast, 29, 55
slavery, 19. *See also* African slaves

Snipes, Wesley, 82
son, 32, 36, 43, 86
Soviet Union, 37
Spain, 41, 50, 70
Spanish dance, 27
Spanish language, 15
street fighting, 80, 82–83
sugarcane, 71, 78
syncopation, 22, 26, 28, 31, 33

T

Tabasco sauce, 86
Taino (Arawak) Indians
    areíto and, 17
    Cuba and, 26–27
    Dominican Republic and, 41
    Haiti and, 50, 52, 53
tangere, 58
tango
    Argentine vs. ballroom, 66–67
    as fusion of African and European dances, 23–24
    habanera, 59–60
    Italianization of, 63–66
    milonga, 60–62
    origin of word, 58–59
    Rudolph Valentino and, 68–69
tango a la francesca, 66–67
tango americano, 59. *See also* Habanera
tango andaluz, 59. *See also* Habanera
Tango Argentino, 65
tango liso, 63
tangomania, 66
tangueros, 65
Ti Ayiti, 56–57
Tjader, Cal, 86
Tordesillas, Treaty of, 70
Torres, Eddie, 39, 89
trade, triangle of, 19

training programs, 40
tres, 32
triangle of trade, 19
trickery, 81
La Tropicana, 36
Troupe Macaya, 53
Trujillo, Petan, 44, 46, 47
Trujillo, Rafael, 42, 44
tumba Francesa, 28
twoubadou songs, 51

U

urbanization, 46

V

vacunano, 33
Valdés, Alfredo Sr., 85
Valentino, 68
Valentino, Rudolph, 68–69
Vargas, Getúlio, 82
Velázquez de Cuéllar, Diego, 26
Ventura, Johnny, 48–49
Vieira, Jelon, 82
viejotecas, 91
vodou dances, 53–57
vodou-djaz, 51
vodoun religion, 25, 51, 52–57
voodoo, 55–56

W

waltz, 19, 51
West Indies, 41
Wilhelm I, 66
Williams, Lavinia, 53

Y

yambú, 35
Yanvalou, 54
Yoruba rhythms, 29, 35

Z

zaka, 55
zapateo, 27–28
Zarenyen, 54, 55
zemba queca, 72
zombies, 56

ABOUT THE AUTHOR

Author **Margaret Musmon** holds BS and MS degrees from Indiana State University and an EdD from Boston University. She is a retired professor and Director of the Dance Program at the University of Massachusetts at Boston, where she coached an award-winning ballroom dance team that competed nationally and internationally. She has edited and produced both the *Dance and the Child International (daCi) Newsletter* and the *Spotlight on Dance* of the National Dance Association. She served as president of the National Dance Association and is president of the Board of Dance Projects, Inc., New York, NY. She served for many years as a member of the scientific committee and on the Board of Conseil Internationale de la Danse, CID-UNESCO. Dr. Musmon has authored numerous articles on dance and given many dance presentations both nationally and internationally. She recently choreographed seven dance pieces performed in Shakespeare's *Twelfth Night*, which was set in the Caribbean. She splits her time between Nahant, Massachusetts, and St. Petersburg, Florida, where she dances with the Rounderettes in the Second Time Arounders Band, the Glitter Sisters, and the Grandmother Rockettes.

ABOUT THE CONSULTING EDITOR

Consulting editor **Elizabeth A. Hanley** is Associate Professor Emerita of Kinesiology at the Pennsylvania State University. She holds a BS in physical education from the University of Maryland and an MS in physical education from the Pennsylvania State University, where she taught such courses as modern dance, figure skating, international folk dance, square and contra dance, and ballroom dance. She is the founder and former director of the Pennsylvania State University International Dance Ensemble and has served as the coordinator of the dance workshop at the International Olympic Academy, in Olympia, Greece.